Law Essential

CRIMINAL LAW

2nd edition

Claire McDiarmid, LL.B., Dip.L.P., LL.M., Ph.D.

Senior Lecturer in Law,
University of Strathclyde

DUNDEE UNIVERSITY PRESS
2010

First edition published in Great Britain in 2007 by
Dundee University Press
University of Dundee
Dundee DD1 4HN

www.dundee.ac.uk/dup

Reprinted 2009
Second edition published 2010

ISBN 1-84586-092-9

No natural forests were destroyed to make this product;
only farmed timber was used and replanted.

British Library Cataloguing-in-Publication Data
A catalogue record for this book is available on request from the British Library

Typeset by Waverley Typesetters, Warham, Norfolk
Printed and bound by CPI Group (UK) Ltd, Croydon, CR0 4YY

CONTENTS

TABLE OF CASES

TABLE OF STATUTES

1 THE DEVELOPMENT OF THE SCOTTISH SYSTEM

SOURCES OF SCOTS CRIMINAL LAW

The primary sources of Scots law generally are, at base: (1) legislation passed by either the Westminster or the Holyrood Parliament; (2) cases previously decided, usually, though not exclusively, by the Scottish courts themselves; and (3) certain 17th-, 18th- and 19th-century texts written by authors of sufficient authority to have acquired the title "institutional writer".

The primary sources of Scots *criminal* law are predominantly cases and institutional writings, though, every year, statutes are passed which create new offences for Scotland. The relative absence of statutory encroachment, however, certainly in the definition of most of the major crimes, means that Scots criminal law is generally said to be based in the common law. All of the major crimes – for example, murder, theft and fireraising – are "common law crimes". In this context, "common law" simply signifies that the law has developed on a case-by-case basis, often from an original definition provided by an institutional writer.

Baron David Hume is the most influential of the institutional writers on the criminal law and it is common to find the High Court of Justiciary making reference to his work today. This is despite the fact that the first edition of his *Commentaries on the Law of Scotland Respecting the Description and Punishment of Crimes* was published in 1797. It was then updated three times, the latest edition appearing in 1844. Though to some extent rather derivative of Hume, Sir Archibald Alison also has the status of an institutional writer, having published his *Principles of the Criminal Law of Scotland* in 1832. Finally, pre-dating both Hume and Alison, Sir George Mackenzie of Rosehaugh produced his *Laws and Customes* [sic] *of Scotland in Matters Criminal* in 1678. Works of these three authors constitute primary sources of criminal law.

Two other writers are referred to frequently in the opinions of the High Court, though their works do not have the status of institutional writings. They are Sir John H A Macdonald, whose *Practical Treatise on the Criminal Law of Scotland* was first published in 1867, proceeding through a further four editions, the fifth and last of which was published in 1948. More recently, Sir Gerald Gordon's *Criminal Law*, known universally as "Gordon", was first published in 1968. The third edition, published in

2001, and written with Michael Christie, is now an important point of reference.

HOW DOES THE LAW DEVELOP?

Criminal law is one of the areas devolved to the Scottish Parliament under the Scotland Act 1998. In other words, it is not a matter reserved to the sole jurisdiction of the Westminster Parliament under Sch 5 to that Act. Accordingly, new offences can be created, or existing ones amended, by an Act of the Parliament in Holyrood. In certain areas, such as the misuse of drugs, the UK Parliament may legislate for the whole of the United Kingdom, including Scotland. In 2003, a group of leading Scottish academics drew up a *Draft Criminal Code for Scotland* which, if ever enacted, would place all of Scots criminal law on a statutory basis. The draft does not simply draw together the existing law but, instead, incorporates proposed amendments, with a view to its improvement and modernisation. The law in the *Code* requires to be discussed and debated before it could be enacted by the Scottish Parliament. At present, therefore, it remains a draft. Accordingly, the courts – and the High Court of Justiciary in particular – continue to play the greater role in developing the criminal law in Scotland.

Court hierarchy and procedure

In Scotland, the onus of proof in criminal cases (almost) always rests on the prosecution. The most minor criminal cases are dealt with in the justice of the peace court. The next tier in the hierarchy is the sheriff court which deals with a very large volume of criminal business, from relatively minor offences (which are heard using *summary procedure*) to matters which are so serious that they require the sheriff to sit with a jury (which is known as *solemn procedure*). Finally, the High Court of Justiciary deals with a few very serious offences at first instance (ie when the case is heard for the first time). These include rape and murder. Such crimes are said to be within its *privative jurisdiction* and are always solemn matters. The High Court is also the main court of appeal in Scotland. This role allows it to play an important part in shaping and developing the criminal law.

The declaratory power

Hume imputes to the High Court "an inherent power … to punish … every act which is obviously of a criminal nature" (i, 12). This is known as the declaratory power and, effectively, it would allow the High Court to create new criminal offences, by declaring to be criminal acts which had not previously been so recognised. It was last used in 1838, in the case of *Bernard Greenhuff and Others* (1838) where it was held that it was a crime to keep a public gaming house for profit. The modern case of *Grant* v *Allan* (1987) seemed to accept that the power still existed but declined to use it.

Human rights

If the power were ever to be used, this would present a particular problem in terms of Art 7 of the European Convention on Human Rights which is headed "No Punishment Without Law". The Article states: "[n]o one shall be held guilty of any criminal offence on account of any act or omission which did not constitute a criminal offence under national or international law at the time when it was committed." Clearly, the declaratory power operates to declare acts criminal retrospectively, in direct contravention of this Article.

Lord Cockburn's dissent in *Greenhuff*

In fact, Lord Cockburn's dissenting judgment in *Greenhuff* has had much more influence over the way in which Scots law has developed since 1838 than the declaratory power itself. On this view of the law, the High Court has power *not* to declare a new crime, but to declare that an existing crime has been committed in a new way, or to declare that conduct which has not been regarded as criminal previously actually falls within already established principles of the criminal law.

In recent years, the High Court has not hesitated to "develop" the law along these lines, in ways which have taken the definition of some crimes well beyond their previously accepted boundaries. This has, however, always been done on the basis of *interpreting* the existing law. The High Court adheres to the principle that it does not, *per se*, make law as this would breach the principle of the separation of powers which requires that law is made by Parliament and only interpreted by the courts. Some examples of this type of radical development include the following:

(1) In 1926, when joyriding first became an issue, the High Court deemed it the crime of "clandestine taking and using": *Strathern* v *Seaforth* (1926).

(2) In 2003, the High Court effectively abolished the existing crime of shameless indecency – which was itself more or less a creation of the courts in the first place: *Webster* v *Dominick* (2003).

(3) In *HM Advocate* v *Purcell* (2008) the High Court added a second strand to the requirements of wicked recklessness. (Wicked recklessness constitutes one of the two *mens rea* for murder). In addition to the existing prerequisite of an utter indifference as to whether the victim lived or died, it stated that there must be an intention to cause personal injury. The matter is now under further consideration in the case of *Petto* v *HM Advocate* (2009).

Codification would ensure that the criminal law was stated clearly and definitively so that every citizen could ascertain easily which acts it proscribed. Legislation has a democratic legitimacy. Development in the courts allows flexibility and the possibility of decisions keeping pace with social developments. There is an ongoing debate as to which is preferable.

Essential Facts

- The main sources of Scots criminal law are institutional writings and cases. An increasing number of statutes also create new offences.
- Hume, Alison and Mackenzie have the status of institutional writers.
- The major crimes in Scots criminal law (eg murder, theft and fireraising) have all, so far, been developed primarily by decisions of the court.
- The High Court is said to have a declaratory power to create new offences. Instead, it generally develops the law by interpreting existing crimes to cover new types of behaviour.
- Article 7 of the European Convention on Human Rights prohibits behaviour being declared criminal retrospectively. It therefore conflicts with the declaratory power.
- A *Draft Criminal Code for Scotland* has been prepared but not enacted.

Essential Cases

Bernard Greenhuff and Others (1838): the last time the High Court's declaratory power was used expressly. Lord Cockburn's dissenting judgment, stating that the High Court's power was, instead, to declare that an existing crime had been committed in a new way, or that apparently new conduct actually fell within existing principles, has been particularly influential.

Grant v Allan (1987): the High Court discussed the existence of the declaratory power but expressly refused to use it.

Strathern v Seaforth (1926): the High Court decided that joyriding was so clearly wrong that it could be relevantly stated to be a crime in Scots law.

Webster v Dominick (2003): the High Court abolished the crime of shameless indecency which it had itself created.

HM Advocate v Purcell (2007): the High Court added a requirement of intention to cause personal injury to the *mens rea* of wicked recklessness for murder.

2 MENTAL AND BEHAVIOURAL ELEMENTS

The definition of all criminal offences consists of a behavioural element and, in most instances, a mental element. The behavioural element is an act which the criminal law prohibits (eg killing another) or an omission where something is required, with which the accused has failed to comply (eg ensuring that dangerous machinery is properly guarded). The mental element is the state of mind which accompanies the behavioural element. The behavioural element is generally referred to as the *actus reus* and the mental element as the *mens rea*.

The *actus reus* and the *mens rea* must occur simultaneously. An act is not criminal unless it is accompanied, at the time of its commission, by the relevant (guilty) state of mind.

THE BEHAVIOURAL ELEMENT

To be convicted of a criminal offence, the accused must be the agent of the harm which is proscribed by the criminal law. In other words, the criminal outcome must have been achieved by behaviour attributable to him or her. He or she must have done, or have omitted do, something contrary to the criminal law. The prosecution must also prove causation – that the accused's action *caused* the harm covered in the definition of the crime.

Voluntary conduct

The criminal law only seeks to punish voluntary actions – or actions which the accused would have been able to avoid committing. In some cases, the accused will nominally have committed an act, or brought about a set of circumstances, but will not, in fact have had any control over this occurrence. If the conduct is completely *involuntary*, the criminal law will not penalise him for it.

Three types of involuntary conduct have been recognised in Scots criminal law:

(1) Weather
In *Hogg* v *Macpherson* (1927), a strong gust of wind blew the accused's furniture van over, causing damage to a lamp standard. It was held that

the accused was not liable to pay compensation to the city of Edinburgh because he had not, in fact, taken any action at all – the damage had all been caused by the wind.

(2) Act of another person

Another person may have been the agent of the harm. In *HM Advocate* v *Hugh Mitchell* (1856) a small child died in her mother's arms because her windpipe had been compressed and she suffocated. Only the child's father was indicted for culpable homicide, however, because it was recognised that it was his violence towards his wife which had actually brought about the child's death. *Mrs* Mitchell had not, in fact, acted at all.

(3) Reflex actions

Although it has not specifically been tested, Scots law appears to accept that a "reflex action" – one which the individual cannot prevent – may be involuntary. This was indicated in *Jessop* v *Johnstone* (1991). In that case, a pupil, leaving a physics class which had been supervised by a PE teacher, hit the teacher with a rolled up jotter. The teacher reacted immediately, by punching the pupil in the back and the stomach. On appeal by the prosecution, the High Court held that this constituted an assault. In the course of its judgment, it suggested that there might well be cases where an individual did react in an instinctive and reflex fashion. Though this case did not fall into this category, it can be inferred from the judgment that such an act would not be regarded as criminal.

In *Johnston* v *NCB* (1960), a civil case, a fly flew into the accused's eye while he was driving a vehicle belonging to his employers along a road on a summer evening. This so surprised him that he lost control of the car and collided with a motorist travelling in the opposite direction. The court stated that "both his eyes [had] closed by involuntary reflex action" (per Lord Kilbrandon at 84). This was enough to establish his negligence under the civil law but the court stated specifically that his actions would not have amounted to a criminal offence.

Omissions

In general, Scots criminal law does not penalise omissions. There is no duty to rescue the victim, nor to prevent the commission of a crime. In *Geo Kerr and Others* (1871), the accused watched an assault taking place but did not participate, nor did he intervene to help the victim. It was held that he had committed no crime. A criminal omission only arises where a legal duty to act exists.

There is little direct Scottish authority on other situations in which omissions become criminal; however, there are thought to be at least two sets of circumstances where this is the case:

(1) Special relationship

If there is a special relationship between the accused and the victim, this can render criminal an omission to act. The most obvious relationship is that between a parent and a child, as discussed in the Australian case of *R v Russell* (1933). This matter has recently been examined in the Scottish case of *Bone* v *HM Advocate* (2006). Here, the accused was the mother of a child who died as a result of injuries inflicted by the mother's partner. He (the partner) was convicted of the child's murder; at first instance, the mother was convicted of the lesser charge of culpable homicide by witnessing and countenancing criminal conduct towards the child by the partner. On appeal by the mother, the High Court stated:

> "[i]n the context of the question whether a parent witnessing an assault on a child could reasonably have acted to protect the child, it is not appropriate to test the matter by reference to a hypothetical reasonable parent; rather the test is whether the particular parent, with all her personal characteristics and in the situation in which she found herself, could reasonably have intervened to prevent the assault" (per Lord Macfadyen at 167).

The court took the view that this particular accused's personal characteristics would have meant that her failure to intervene to protect the child was not unreasonable. Her culpable homicide conviction was accordingly quashed. More generally, this demonstrates that the standard required of a parent in protecting his or her children is not absolute. A criminal omission is only constituted where his or her failure to act was unreasonable taking account, subjectively, of all his or her own personal characteristics at the time of the omission.

Looking at a different type of relationship, the American case of *People* v *Beardsley* (1907) held that the relationship between a man and his mistress was not such as to create a legal duty which would render a failure to act criminal. The mistress had ingested a fatal dose of morphine in the accused's presence and he had failed to prevent her from doing so.

(2) Legal duty

Sometimes a legal duty, the failure to perform which will amount to a criminal omission, is imposed on the accused by her voluntary adoption of the responsibility; or by virtue of a contract into which she has entered; or by a statute.

(a) **Voluntary adoption of responsibility.** An example of voluntary adoption is the English case of *R* v *Instan* (1893). Here, it was held that a niece was properly convicted of manslaughter where she lived with her aunt, and had no income of her own. The niece failed to provide food for her aunt or to seek medical attention for her during the last 10 days of her life when the aunt was confined to bed with gangrene and unable to move. It is slightly unclear why the court determined that the clear *moral* obligation on the niece should be translated into a legal duty. Part of the answer is that the niece continued to accept food deliveries to the house from various tradespeople, from which she ate herself and which were paid for by her aunt. The niece also had many opportunities to seek assistance for her aunt but failed to do so.

(b) **Contractual duty.** A similar legal duty was held to have been created by a contract of employment in *HM Advocate* v *William Hardie* (1847). In this case, a woman, who was in receipt of "relief" (the equivalent of benefits) from the Parish Board in Falkirk became ill and made a number of applications for further sums to be paid to her. William Hardie, the assistant inspector of the poor to whom these applications were passed, seems to have ignored them. The woman subsequently died. The court held that it was competent to charge Hardie with culpable homicide for his neglect of duty in failing properly to process her applications, or to get her "an adequate supply of the necessaries of life" (at 249). No further proceedings were, however, taken in the case.

(c) **Statute.** Statutes sometimes impose positive obligations with criminal sanctions where these are not carried out. For example, a police officer may require a person suspected of driving under the influence of drink or drugs to provide a specimen of breath, blood or urine under s 7 of the Road Traffic Act 1988.

Prior dangerous act?

Until the High Court decision in *McCue* v *Currie* (2004), it had been widely thought that, where an accused's actions created a dangerous situation which she then failed to make safe, that omission could constitute the behavioural element of a criminal offence. Thus, in *HM Advocate* v *McPhee* (1935), the accused assaulted a woman and left her lying unconscious outside overnight in inclement weather. She later died. Leaving her exposed to the elements, instead of seeking medical attention for her, (in addition to the assault) allowed him to be indicted for murder. Similarly, in *MacPhail* v *Clark* (1983), a farmer set fire to some straw and allowed the smoke to drift across a road affecting visibility so badly that two vehicles collided. He was found guilty of culpably and recklessly endangering the lieges: having set the fire he should have realised that it would cause thick smoke on the public highway (this amounted to recklessness) *and* he then took no steps to extinguish it. In other words, he omitted to make the dangerous situation safe.

MacPhail v *Clark* is a sheriff court decision. *McCue* v *Currie*, a High Court appeal, however, indicates that the omission to make safe a danger of the accused's own creation is not (or not yet) a criminal offence in Scots law. In the case, the accused had broken into a caravan in Kilmarnock and had stolen a bottle of Bacardi and some kitchen utensils. He was using a cigarette lighter for illumination and, when he had taken what he wanted, the lighter burst in his hand so he dropped it. The caravan caught fire but the accused did not stay to establish what would happen. He certainly made no attempt to extinguish the fire, which he had started, and render it safe. The court expressly considered *MacPhail* v *Clark* but still reached the conclusion that the accused's actions did not amount to a crime. The judgment did, however, state that "it may be that there is a case for enacting a new crime, ..., of culpably failing to take appropriate steps after a situation of danger to persons or property has arisen as a result of a person's actings" (at 80, per Temporary Judge C G B Nicolson).

Causation

The second aspect of the behavioural element, beyond the act or omission itself, is causation. The prosecution must prove a direct link between the accused's conduct and, in result crimes, the requisite result. (Result crimes are crimes which are only constituted if a particular result occurs. Murder and culpable homicide are the most obvious examples, where the "result" is the death of the victim.)

In general, causation only presents a difficulty where a number of causes have contributed to the final outcome. In that event, the court will have to decide whether the accused's action was the operating cause of the harm. For example, if the accused shoots the complainer and the complainer dies instantly from the wounds inflicted, it is clear that the accused's act was the cause of the death. If, on the other hand, the accused shoots the victim who survives but, on the way to hospital, the ambulance is involved in a road accident which causes other injuries and the victim is found to be dead on arrival at hospital, it may be much less clear that the accused did "cause" the death.

The "eggshell skull" rule

In examining questions of causation, Scots law utilises the "eggshell skull" rule. This means that the accused must take the victim as she finds him. If the victim has an "eggshell skull", which shatters at the slightest tap causing death, then the accused is equally responsible for the victim's death, if she has inflicted that tap, as if she had repeatedly assaulted the victim with a knife or a baseball bat. This principle is also sometimes referred to as "taking your victim as you find him".

In *Bird* v *HM Advocate* (1952), the accused was convicted of culpable homicide. He suspected a woman of stealing money from him and he had, therefore, followed her along a road. Eventually, he pulled her from a passing car, to stop her getting away. She collapsed and died. It was established that she had had a diseased heart and had died from emotional shock caused by the accused. The fact that her heart was much weaker than might have been expected was irrelevant. The accused had assaulted her (though the court acknowledged that the attack was very minor) and she died as a result. He had to take her as he found her and he was, therefore, responsible for her death.

Novus actus interveniens

A *novus actus interveniens* breaks the chain of causation so that the accused ceases to be responsible for outcomes which follow on from it. The question is usually whether the ultimate outcome was a foreseeable result of the action taken by the accused – in which case she or he is responsible for it – or whether it was totally unpredictable – in which case it is a *novus actus interveniens*.

Actions taken by the victim will not always constitute a *novus actus interveniens*. For example, in *Khaliq* v *HM Advocate* (1984), the accused sold glue-sniffing kits to children. In determining a plea to the relevancy of the indictment, the High Court held that his knowledge that the kits would be used for this harmful purpose would be enough to establish causation between his act in selling the kits and any injury suffered by the children in using them. It would not be a *novus actus interveniens* that the children had to ingest the toxic fumes before harm would result to them. The court seems to have been particularly influenced by the fact that the solvent was provided in a receptacle from which it could be inhaled, thus indicating that the accused must have known what the ultimate use would be. This approach to causation has recently been affirmed by the High Court in *MacAngus and Kane* v *HM Advocate* (2009).

THE MENTAL ELEMENT

Each crime has its own *mens rea* which is apparent from examining its definition. (Definitions are derived from the leading cases or, in statutory offences, set down in the relevant legislation.) The Latin maxim *actus non facit reum nisi mens sit rea* is the basis of the Scottish approach to *mens rea*. Roughly translated, it means that there can be no criminal act without a criminal mind.

Dole

The traditional Scottish approach to *mens rea* required "dole" – from the Latin "*dolus*" meaning evil. Dole, as defined by Hume, is an all-encompassing concept relating to the wickedness of the character of the accused person. Some cases still make reference to "dole", sometimes in the technical sense used by Hume; in other cases simply as an alternative to the term *mens rea*.

Motive

In general, motive is irrelevant. The criminal law does not ask *why* the accused committed the crime. In *Quinn* v *Lees* (1994) a man set his dog on some boys, apparently as a joke. The court held that, when the accused ordered his dog to "fetch", that was a deliberate action thereby satisfying the *mens rea* requirement of evil intent in a charge of assault. The joke issue related to the accused's alleged motive in acting in that way and was therefore irrelevant.

Proof of the mental element

Proof of the mental element usually has to be by inference from the surrounding circumstances. This is because it is impossible to read the mind of another person. Thus, although *mens rea* is expressed *subjectively*, as the accused's own personal mental attitude, *proof* of *mens rea* really has to be *objective*. That is to say, on examining the surrounding circumstances, it is reasonable to infer that the accused had a particular mental attitude towards her actions at the time.

Forms of *mens rea*

The three most common forms of *mens rea* are intention (to do something criminal), recklessness (effectively, gross indifference as to the consequences of one's actions) and knowledge (about some aspect of the act – for example, in reset, knowledge that the goods were stolen). These are not stand-alone concepts however, nor are they interchangeable. They only have meaning where they form part of the definition of specific criminal offences and each criminal offence has its own, individually defined, *mens rea*.

Absence of mental element: error

If the accused has made an error, the effect of this may be that he does not, in fact, have the necessary knowledge or intention and, therefore, that the Crown is unable to prove the *mens rea* element of the offence.

Errors of law

Errors of law are irrelevant: "ignorance of the law is no excuse". Generally, people are deemed to know the law whether or not they do so in fact.

Errors of fact

If an error of fact is extreme, to the extent that it negates *mens rea* or that it justifies the accused's otherwise illegal actions, it may allow the accused to be acquitted. The court usually has to be satisfied that it was reasonable, in the circumstances, for the accused to have made the error. For example, in *Dewar* v *HM Advocate* (1945), the accused, a crematorium manager, was convicted of the theft of two coffins and around 1,000 coffin lids. His defence was that he thought his actions were legal because the coffin lids had been abandoned and were, therefore, not owned by anyone. It was held that this was wrong in terms of the law of property – the coffin lids did have owners. However, the *mens rea* of theft is the intention to deprive the owner of her property. Strictly, then, because Dewar thought the coffins and lids did not have an owner, he could not have the necessary intention. If taken at face value, his error would negate the *mens rea*. In fact, though, in charging the jury at the trial, the judge stated that Dewar would have had to establish "reasonable grounds, rational grounds, colourable grounds" (at 9) for holding this belief, before it could exonerate him. On appeal, the High Court took the view that this expressed the position in the most favourable way possible to the accused. Thus, certainly in the law of theft, an error as to fact must be held on reasonable grounds before it will exonerate an accused person.

Other areas of the criminal law also require errors to be made on reasonable grounds, for example, self-defence in murder: *Owens* v *HM Advocate* (1946). Again, s 1(1) of the Sexual Offences (Scotland) Act 2009 requires that, if the accused's defence to rape is that he thought that the victim consented to the sexual intercourse, this belief must be held on reasonable grounds.

Essential Facts

- All crimes have a behavioural element (the *actus reus*) and (usually) a mental element (the *mens rea*).

- The *actus reus* and the *mens rea* must occur simultaneously.

- The *actus reus* may be constituted by an act or by an omission.

- Only voluntary acts are punishable by the criminal law. Where the accused was unable to avoid the criminal behaviour (as where, for example, it was caused by the weather, or by the act of another person, or by a reflex action) he will not be criminally liable.

- The general rule is that an omission to act is not criminal. There is no duty to rescue.

- Omissions only become criminal where there is a special relationship (such as parent and child) between the accused and the victim or where there is a legal duty imposed on the accused by voluntary adoption of the responsibility, or by virtue of a contract, or by a statute.

- It must be proven that the accused's act caused the criminal outcome. Scots law uses the "eggshell skull" rule. This means that, in an assault case, the accused is responsible for all of the physical consequences to the victim of their actions, regardless of the victim's existing state of health. The accused must "take the victim as they find him".

- A "*novus actus interveniens*" interrupts the chain of causation and ends the accused's criminal liability for the act.

- The *mens rea* is the criminal state of mind which accompanies the criminal act.

- Motive is usually irrelevant.

Essential Cases

Geo Kerr and Others (1871): observing a crime and failing to intervene to help the victim is not, in itself, criminal.

Bird v HM Advocate (1952): the accused must take his victim as he finds him or her. Pre-existing medical conditions which exacerbate injuries inflicted by the accused do not lessen his guilt.

Quinn v Lees (1994): motive is irrelevant.

Dewar v HM Advocate (1945): in theft, an error must be held on reasonable grounds before it will provide a defence.

3 CRIMES AGAINST PROPERTY

In Scots criminal law, there are three crimes which are committed against property: malicious mischief, vandalism and fireraising.

MALICIOUS MISCHIEF

Actus reus

The *actus reus* of malicious mischief is damage to, or destruction of, the property of another person.

The accused must damage, or physically injure, property belonging to another person. The type of property included is wide ranging. In *Clark* v *Syme* (1957), the accused was convicted of malicious mischief for shooting his neighbour's sheep.

The degree of damage caused may be very slight. In *Ward* v *Robertson* (1938), the three accused were charged with malicious mischief for walking across a grass field where sheep were grazing. The "damage" was to the grass itself, the walking having, allegedly, rendered it unfit for consumption by sheep. If the accused had done this maliciously (which they did not), this would have been sufficient to establish the *actus reus*.

"Wilson-*type" malicious mischief: patrimonial loss*

Until 1983, the elements of the *actus reus* of malicious mischief were clear. The case of *HM Advocate* v *Wilson* (1983), however, departed from the principle that actual physical damage to property is, in every case, necessary. In *Wilson*, the accused activated an emergency stop button at Hunterston B power station. This stopped electricity being fed into the national grid for 28 hours, leading to losses of around £147,000. All that the accused had done was to press the button. The court held that, because this had been done maliciously, and because it had caused financial loss, this was sufficient to satisfy the requirements of the crime.

Subsequent to *Wilson*, an attempt was made to expand the law of malicious mischief still further. In *Bett* v *Hamilton* (1997), the accused was charged with maliciously moving a surveillance camera so that it pointed away from the front of a bank. This was alleged to have wasted running costs and to have exposed the bank to a greater risk of theft and vandalism. The court held that this was not a crime. Malicious mischief required *either* damage to property *or* patrimonial loss. Here, the bank had suffered no financial loss whatsoever; therefore, the charge failed to disclose a crime known to Scots law.

Mens rea

The *mens rea* of malicious mischief requires a deliberate and wicked intention to damage the property of another. Alternatively, the crime can be committed with a "deliberate disregard of, or even indifference to, the property or possessory rights of others" (*Ward* v *Robertson* (1938), per Lord Justice-Clerk Aitchison at 36) – in other words, recklessly.

VANDALISM

Vandalism is a statutory offence. This means that its full definition is to be found in the statute in which it is set down. Vandalism is contained in s 52 of the Criminal Law (Consolidation) (Scotland) Act 1995. As an offence, it is not dissimilar to malicious mischief. *Black* v *Allan* (1985), however, specifically held that vandalism was an offence in its own right and not "simply an echo" (per Lord Justice-General Emslie at 12) of the crime of malicious mischief.

Actus reus

The criminal act required is the destruction or damage of property belonging to another, without reasonable excuse.

Without reasonable excuse

The Crown must specifically prove, beyond reasonable doubt, that the accused acted "without reasonable excuse". In other words, if the accused had an excuse which the law regards as reasonable, he or she must be acquitted. It is for the judge to decide, in each case, whether an excuse is reasonable. In *MacDougall* v *Ho* (1985), the proprietor of a Chinese takeaway damaged the windscreen of a taxi because he believed (wrongly) that a person who had just broken his shop window was escaping in it. This was held to constitute a reasonable excuse.

Mens rea

The destruction or damage must have been carried out either "wilfully" (ie intentionally) or recklessly.

In defining recklessness, vandalism draws on the way in which the general criminal law deals with this concept. In *Black* v *Allan* (1985), the three accused had been involved in horseplay in the course of which one accused had jumped onto, and then been thrown off, the back of another – straight through the front window of the Clydesdale Bank in Penicuik. The magistrate who convicted the accused had not considered whether the horseplay created an obvious and material risk of damage (the then test for recklessness in Scots law generally) to the window, so the High Court held that it was impossible to determine whether the accused had acted recklessly. The convictions were quashed.

Vandalism and wilful fireraising

Acts of wilful fireraising cannot constitute vandalism.

FIRERAISING

There are three crimes of fireraising in Scots common law: (a) wilful fireraising; (b) culpable and reckless fireraising; and (c) fireraising to defraud insurers.

Wilful, and culpable and reckless, fireraising: *actus reus*

The distinction between wilful fireraising and culpable and reckless fireraising rests entirely in the *mens rea*. The *actus reus* is the same for both. It consists in setting fire to any type of corporeal property, so long as it belongs to another and the accused does not have the owner's consent. (The concept of corporeal property is discussed in Chapter 4: Crimes of Dishonesty.)

The fire must actually have taken hold of the property but it can be set directly or indirectly. In *Carr* v *HM Advocate* (1994), the appellant set fire to a roll of paper towels which he had scrunched up. This in turn set fire to the curtains and, ultimately, the building. The court held that if it could be inferred from the appellant's conduct and the circumstances of his act that he intended to set fire to the building itself, this would be enough to constitute wilful fireraising of the building, even though he had directly applied the fire only to the paper towels.

Wilful fireraising

Mens rea

Wilful fireraising is the more serious offence. The *mens rea* is an actual intention to damage or destroy the property which the accused has ignited. In *Byrne* v *HM Advocate* (2000), the accused set fire to some paper on the floor of a building owned by a housing association in

Dundee. The fire then took effect on the building itself. At first instance, the accused was convicted of wilful fireraising. On appeal, the five-judge court held that, in order to convict of wilful fireraising, the Crown must establish that the accused actually intended to burn the relevant property. If this was not possible, perhaps because the accused's intention extended only to the item of property which he had initially ignited, only a conviction for culpable and reckless fireraising would be possible. Wilful fireraising could not be committed recklessly. Byrne's conviction was quashed.

There is no scope for any doctrine of transferred intent. If the accused set fire to curtains, and his only intention was to burn the curtains, he is guilty only of wilful fireraising of the curtains. If the building burns, he may be guilty of culpable and reckless fireraising of the building but the intent as regards the curtains cannot be "transferred" to the building.

An accused who is charged with wilful fireraising can be convicted of culpable and reckless fireraising only if the charge specifically states this as an alternative.

Culpable and reckless fireraising

Mens rea
To be convicted of culpable and reckless fireraising, "mere negligence is not enough: the property must have been set on fire due to an act of the accused displaying a reckless disregard as to what the result of his act would be" (*Byrne* v *HM Advocate* (2000), per Lord Coulsfield at 163). Recklessness, in this context, basically means that the accused's actions show "a complete disregard for any dangers which might result from what he was doing" (*Carr* v *HM Advocate* (1994), per Lord Justice-General Hope at 208). It should be noted that this definition of recklessness applies specifically to cases of culpable and reckless fireraising.

The case of *McCue* v *Currie* (2004), where the accused set fire to a caravan in Kilmarnock, takes a very narrow view of the way in which recklessness is to be conceptualised. In that case, the accused accidentally dropped the cigarette lighter which he had been using for illumination, then immediately left the caravan, which subsequently burned. On appeal, the High Court held that recklessness could be inferred only from the appellant's actions in starting the fire. In other words, it could look only at the exact moment at which he dropped the lighter. At that point, it was accepted that he was not reckless – he dropped the lighter accidentally because it was burning his hand. While his subsequent failure to do anything to prevent the fire may have been reckless, this was irrelevant because, at the moment when the fire was raised, he did not have the requisite *mens rea* for culpable and reckless fireraising.

Fireraising to defraud insurers

This crime usually consists in setting fire to one's own property. The act must have been carried out with the intention of defrauding an insurer but it is not necessary that the fraudulent claim has actually been submitted. If the fire has been raised and the fraudulent scheme is obvious, this is sufficient. An example is *Sutherland* v *HM Advocate* (1994).

Essential Facts

- Malicious mischief is constituted by damage to, or destruction of, the property of another person which is carried out deliberately and wickedly (intentionally) or with deliberate disregard or indifference to the property rights of others (recklessly).

- The type of property which can be the subject of the crime is wide ranging and the damage may be very slight.

- *HM Advocate* v *Wilson* (1983) extended the *actus reus* to include patrimonial (financial or economic) loss. *Bett* v *Hamilton* (1997) declined to widen it any further.

- Section 52 of the Criminal Law (Consolidation) (Scotland) Act 1995 defines vandalism as the wilful or reckless destruction of, or damage to, the property of another, without reasonable excuse.

- Acts of wilful fireraising cannot constitute vandalism.

- The *actus reus* of wilful, and of culpable and reckless, fireraising is the same: setting fire to the corporeal property of another without his or her consent.

- The fire must actually have taken hold of the property but this may be achieved directly or indirectly.

- The *mens rea* of wilful fireraising is the intention to damage or destroy the specific item of property which the accused has ignited.

- Intention cannot be transferred from one item to another.

- The *mens rea* of culpable and reckless fireraising is a reckless disregard by the accused as to the outcome of his or her act.

- The question of whether or not the accused has acted recklessly can be judged by reference only to the moment when he or she set the fire.
- Fireraising to defraud insurers arises where the accused sets fire (usually) to his or her own property as part of a fraudulent scheme against an insurer.

Essential Cases

HM Advocate v Wilson (1983): explains the principles of malicious mischief, interpreting (or extending) the crime so that it can be constituted where only financial loss is caused.

Byrne v HM Advocate (2000): redefines wilful fireraising and draws a clear distinction from culpable and reckless fireraising.

4 CRIMES OF DISHONESTY

THEFT

The purpose of the crime of theft is to protect people's rights of property in moveable items. It has always been regarded as a serious crime. Indeed, it was originally a capital crime.

What type of property can be stolen?

To be capable of being stolen, property must be moveable, corporeal and in the ownership of someone else.

(1) Moveable

"Moveable" means capable of being moved around. It is impossible to steal land or the things which attach to land, such as buildings. Crops and trees can be stolen only once they have been harvested or otherwise detached from the ground in which they grow.

(2) Corporeal

"Corporeal" means things which can be touched and held, although, because it can be appropriated, charges of theft of electricity have been libelled.

Theft of information. A difficulty arises in relation to information, which is incorporeal and therefore not stealable. It is possible to steal the item holding the information – for example, a memory stick – but its value may be minimal by comparison with the information itself.

In the case of *Dewar* (1777), an apprentice broke into his employer's office, removed a book containing trade secrets, copied them and then returned the book. He was charged with theft by housebreaking but convicted of an innominate offence, thereby escaping the death penalty.

Similarly, in *HM Advocate v Mackenzies* (1913), there were two charges – one of theft of a book of secret trade recipes, and the other of making copies of the recipes with the intention of selling them. The second charge was dismissed as irrelevant. This indicates that the taking of information is not, in itself, criminal.

Neither *Dewar* nor *Mackenzies*, then, supports the proposition that incorporeal property can be stolen.

The modern case of *Grant* v *Allan* (1987) has held that it is not a crime dishonestly to exploit confidential information. The accused had taken a copy of confidential computer print-outs containing lists of his employer's business customers and had offered to sell it to someone else. The High Court held that this was not a crime known to the law of Scotland, nor was such behaviour so obviously of a criminal nature that it should declare it to be a crime. The employer should have sued in the civil courts.

(3) In the ownership of another

The stolen thing must be in the ownership of another. It is not possible to steal your own property.

If the owner of the thing agreed to transfer the right of property to the alleged thief, this could not constitute theft. The thing must be taken without the owner's consent.

There is no requirement for the thief to profit from the theft.

Actus reus

The essence of the *actus reus* of theft is appropriation. Appropriation occurs where the thief comes into possession of the goods lawfully, but subsequently forms the intention dishonestly to retain them.

There is an overlap between the *actus reus* and the *mens rea* of theft. The moment when the crime is committed is the moment when the thief decides dishonestly to keep the thing. Since this is something which happens entirely in his or her own mind, it may be difficult for the prosecution to prove.

Usually, the dishonest intention will have to be inferred from the surrounding circumstances. For example, if the thief sold the thing, that would create the necessary inference that he intended permanently to deprive the owner of it.

Dewar v *HM Advocate* (1945) was the case where the crematorium manager stole two coffins and a number of coffin lids, on the mistaken view that they had been abandoned and were, therefore, no longer in anyone's ownership. The court held that the removal of the coffin lids was enough to give evidence of his theftuous intent. The moment when the lids were removed was, therefore, the moment when appropriation took place. It should be noted that, in his position as crematorium manager, Dewar had clearly come into possession of the coffin lids lawfully.

In *Black* v *Carmichael* (1992), the High Court held that, provided that the Crown could prove the relevant facts, wheel-clamping a car on private property and refusing to release it until a payment was made could amount to both theft and extortion. With regard to theft, the vehicle was appropriated at the moment when the wheel clamp was applied to it. At that moment, the owner of the car had been intentionally deprived of the possession and control of his vehicle.

In this instance, the wheel-clampers did not take the car away. The car-owner was deprived only of possession and control. Deprivation of *any* of the rights of ownership, then, appears to be sufficient to constitute theft. The thief does not have to remove the property completely.

Amotio
Amotio, as a form of the *actus reus* of theft, arises if an object is physically moved in a way which shows an intention to steal it. Gordon suggests that it can occur whenever the thief simply moves something from its place such as from one room to another (para 14-11).

Containers. If the thing is in a container, such as a pocket or a drawer, it must be physically removed from that container before there is *amotio*.

Self-service shops. It is theoretically theft to take something off the shelf with the intention of not paying for it, as in *Barr v O'Brien* (1991), where the accused took two computer tapes off a shelf and placed them in his pocket. He walked past all but the last check-out before realising that he was being watched, whereupon he turned round and went back to the middle of the shop with the tapes still in his pocket. The High Court held that sufficient had been alleged here to make theft a relevant charge.

Finding
A person who finds property and holds on to it may be said to have demonstrated the intention of keeping it and thus to have committed theft.

In *MacMillan v Lowe* (1991), the accused found several cheque books and cheque cards and attempted to conceal them from the police. The High Court took the view that, even though a relatively short time had passed since the finding (4 hours), there was enough from which to infer that the thief had appropriated the items.

Part VI of the Civic Government (Scotland) Act 1982 makes specific statutory provisions in respect of lost and abandoned property, including a requirement that a person who finds goods should report this to the police within a reasonable time.

Mens rea

Intention to deprive permanently. The *mens rea* of theft can best be defined as the intention to deprive the owner of his property. This intention will be inferred from the facts. Until the 1970s, it was necessary to demonstrate that the accused intended to deprive the owner of their goods *permanently*. Later judgments have, however, broadened the scope of the *mens rea*.

In *Kivlin v Milne* (heard 1974, reported 1979), a car was taken without the owner's consent and abandoned. The High Court approved the inference, drawn by the sheriff, of intention to deprive permanently, because it had been left in a place in which the owner was unlikely to find it. This broadened the circumstances in which the *mens rea* of intention to deprive permanently could be inferred.

Intention to deprive temporarily. In 1981, the case of *Milne v Tudhope* developed the law in this area even further. The owner of a cottage was dissatisfied with building works and asked the builders to carry out remedial work free of charge. They refused to do so without payment. Without the owner's consent, they removed various items from the premises, including radiators, a boiler and a number of doors, intending to "hold them to ransom" until payment for the requested remedial work was made. They were convicted of theft and appealed. The main issue in the appeal was whether the *mens rea* of theft was sufficiently made out where the intention was to deprive the owner of his property only temporarily. The High Court agreed with a statement made by the sheriff at first instance that "in certain exceptional cases an intention to deprive temporarily will suffice" (per Lord Justice-Clerk Wheatley at 57).

The judgment affirmed a view expressed by Macdonald, in the first edition of his book in 1867, that, if the intention is to deprive only temporarily, the taking of the items must be clandestine and for a nefarious purpose. "Clandestine", the court held, means secret so far as the owner of the goods is concerned. The things may be taken in open view of the general public but, if the owner did not know that this had happened, it is still a clandestine taking for the purposes of the law of theft. The requirement of nefariousness was here satisfied by the fact that the principal accused must have known that his actions were unlawful.

Thus, the law of theft moved away from the requirement that the thief must intend to deprive the owner of his property permanently. It is now sufficient if there is:

(1) an intention to deprive temporarily; and

(2) a clandestine appropriation; and

(3) a nefarious purpose.

The court in *Milne* v *Tudhope* also stated that the intention to deprive temporarily could only be held to exist in certain exceptional cases. The implication is that other cases should be similarly exceptional before this form of *mens rea* could be made out.

Unfortunately, subsequent cases, while apparently accepting that the intention to deprive temporarily is sufficient, have not provided guidance as to what is necessary to make the circumstances attending a theft "clandestine", "nefarious" and "exceptional". In *Kidston* v *Annan* (1984) the owner of a broken television set answered an advertisement in a newspaper offering free estimates prior to repairs being carried out. The accused, who had placed the advert, did not provide a telephone estimate but, instead, refused to return the set unless its owner paid him £12.50 for repairs which he claimed actually to have completed. He was convicted of theft. On appeal, the High Court held that he had been holding the set to ransom similarly to the circumstances of *Milne* v *Tudhope*. The court took the view that the accused's actions were "nefarious" because he seemed to have lied to the sheriff about having authority to carry out the repair. Beyond this, however, the case does not discuss when the intention to deprive only temporarily will be enough to constitute the *mens rea* of theft.

In *Black* v *Carmichael* (1992) (the wheel-clamping case) there was also temporary appropriation – the intention would have been to return the possessory rights to the owner when he paid the clamping fee. The judges appear to accept that the intention to deprive temporarily is sufficient but there is no discussion of the three additional conditions which *Milne* v *Tudhope* attached. The fact that the accuseds' actions were held to amount to extortion may be sufficient to imply nefariousness.

Intention to deprive indefinitely. The law has continued to develop with the case of *Fowler* v *O'Brien* (1994), where the accused stole a bicycle. He had previously asked the owner if he could borrow it, and the owner had refused. The accused then simply took the bicycle but did not say whether, or when, he would return it. The High Court found this to be a relevant charge of theft, describing the *mens rea* as the intention to deprive the owner of his property indefinitely. The court held that this was different from an intention to deprive temporarily and that, therefore, there was no need to establish that the case was exceptional or that the taking was clandestine and for a nefarious purpose.

Overall, the question arising is, therefore, whether the qualifications on the *mens rea*, where the intention is to deprive temporarily, still apply? *Fowler* v *O'Brien* seems to suggest that they do; *Black* v *Carmichael* that a simple intention to deprive is enough.

AGGRAVATED FORMS OF THEFT

Theft by housebreaking

This is the major aggravation of theft. The housebreaking must be committed *before* the theft, and be the means by which the theft takes place.

"House"

Housebreaking may be committed against any roofed building, provided that it is shut and fast against intruders.

"Breaking"

Breaking includes any means by which the security of the building is overcome. Thus, if the thief uses skeleton or stolen keys, this constitutes the crime. If the building is *not*, actually, shut and fast, and the thief takes advantage of that, this is not theft by housebreaking. Accordingly, if the householder had left the key in the lock, and the thief simply turned it, that would not constitute housebreaking. Entering through an open ground-floor window would, however, probably constitute housebreaking, because that is not a normal means of entry.

There must be evidence that the "house" was secure before the house-breaking took place. This could not be established in *Lafferty* v *Wilson* (1990).

Housebreaking with intent to steal

Housebreaking is not a criminal offence in itself. It is the theft element which renders it criminal. If nothing has actually been stolen, however, it may still be possible to charge the accused with housebreaking with *intent* to steal. There would need to be facts from which this intent could be inferred.

In *Burns* v *Allan* (1987), the accused was caught running away from a building, carrying housebreakers' tools. The burglar alarm had gone off, apparently because the accused had been trying to disconnect it. He was convicted of attempted housebreaking with intent to steal and appealed. The High Court affirmed the sheriff's view that a burglar alarm is integral to the security of any building and that, by disconnecting it, the accused had attempted to overcome that security. His intent to steal could be inferred because it was unlikely that he would be found in those circumstances if he had a lawful purpose.

It is only the intent to *steal* which makes housebreaking a criminal offence. Housebreaking with the intent to commit another crime is not recognised as criminal. In *HM Advocate* v *Forbes* (1994), the accused was charged with housebreaking with intent to commit rape. The High Court held that there was no such crime. Instead, it gave leave for the prosecutor to amend the charge to one of breach of the peace. In *Cochrane* v *HM Advocate* (2006), the High Court accepted that conspiracy merely to break into a house was not a crime known to the law of Scotland. There must also be an allegation that the purpose of the housebreaking was intent to steal.

Theft by opening lockfast places

Theft by opening lockfast places consists in breaking into anything which is secured by a lock, other than a building – for example, a car. Breaking into individual rooms within a building is a further example.

PREVENTIVE OFFENCES

"Preventive" offences criminalise behaviour which takes place in preparation for the commission of a crime. Two of the main preventive offences are found in ss 57 and 58 of the Civic Government (Scotland) Act 1982. The wording of these sections does not suggest that there is any need for *mens rea* as such. The intention to commit theft has to be inferred but there is no requirement for the accused to intend to be on the relevant premises (s 57) or to know that he is, or intends to be, in possession of the relevant tools (s 58). The statute provides a possible defence to each of the offences.

Section 57 – being in premises with intent to commit theft

Section 57 criminalises being found in or on premises (or in a vehicle or vessel) in circumstances from which an intention to commit theft could reasonably be inferred. If the accused can show that he or she had lawful authority to be there, that is a valid defence. In *Marr* v *Heywood* (1993), a burglar alarm went off, alerting the householder to an attempted break-in at the premises. He found the accused scrambling into the garden of a neighbouring house. When the accused was arrested, he said "I didn't get into the house, you can't do me with this" (at 1255). The intent to steal was inferred.

The importance of the intention to commit theft was highlighted in the case of *Wilson v Barbour* (2009). The accused was a 20-year-old student and an expert free-climber. He was found in an eye clinic in Aberdeen, asleep in a cupboard. He had been drinking heavily and had apparently climbed the drainpipe and entered through an unlocked window on the second floor in order to find somewhere to sleep. It was held that this was not enough of a factual basis on which to infer an intention to steal.

Section 58 – convicted thief in possession (of tools)

Section 58 only applies to someone with at least two previous convictions for theft. It criminalises possession of a tool, from which an intention to commit theft could reasonably be inferred. To use the defence, the accused must demonstrate satisfactorily that the possession is *not* for the purposes of theft. In *Allan* v *Bree* (1987), the accused was observed by the police, on two occasions, in and near a car park, skulking in undergrowth and scrutinising cars through binoculars. He had two previous convictions for theft. He had with him the binoculars, two torches and a pair of gloves. The court held that he had no case to answer. The "theftuous intention" had to be inferred from the tools themselves – not from the surrounding circumstances. Binoculars, a torch and gloves are not suspicious in themselves.

RESET

Reset involves the possession of property, knowing that it has been dishonestly obtained. The same person cannot be convicted of both theft and reset of the same goods.

Actus reus

The *actus reus* of reset is the retention of the stolen goods. Absolutely minimal possession will be sufficient, so long as the necessary *mens rea* can be inferred. In *Robert Finlay and Others* (1826), the goods were thrown onto a bed in a room in the house of one of the accused. The accused then threw a cover over them and jumped out of the window. This was sufficient to constitute the possession necessary for reset. His concealment of the goods allowed the court to infer his guilty knowledge of their origin. Note that, as with theft, this creates the difficulty of the overlap of the *actus reus* with the *mens rea*.

At least, in *Finlay*, it was clear that the accused did have possession of the goods, however briefly. Macdonald, however, stated that "it is reset for a person to connive at a third party possessing or retaining stolen goods even if the person charged never laid a finger on the property stolen" (67).

The "connivance at" form of the *actus reus* has been used in relation to people who have allowed themselves to be driven in cars which they know to be stolen and where stolen items have been placed in cars. In *McCawley* (1959), the accused was convicted of reset in respect of his having been one of several passengers in a stolen car. He had fled when police stopped the car, thereby implying the guilty knowledge that he was privy to the retention of the stolen car. The case expressly affirms that being privy to the retention of the stolen property is sufficient to constitute the *actus reus* of reset.

Mens rea

The *mens rea* of reset has two requirements:

(1) the knowledge that the goods are stolen or otherwise dishonestly obtained. It is a definite requirement, set down by Hume (i, 114), that there should be actual knowledge that the goods are stolen, rather than mere suspicion that that is the case; and

(2) the intention to deprive the owner of the goods.

Proof of this knowledge will usually come from the incriminating circumstances surrounding the discovery of the goods.

In *Forbes* v *HM Advocate* (1994) the goods consisted of a valuable painting which was in a 3-foot by 4-foot parcel found in the accused's car. The accused stated that he did not know that the cardboard packaging contained a painting nor how it could have got there. He also gave an "awkward story" about the circumstances in which he came to be driving his car at all that day. He was convicted of reset.

On the other hand, in *Shannon* v *HM Advocate* (1985) the accused was found in possession of a sawn-off shotgun. His conviction for reset was overturned because he might have been attempting to conceal the gun simply because he knew that to have it constituted a breach of the firearms legislation.

Doctrine of recent possession

The doctrine of recent possession applies to both theft and reset. If the goods are found in the accused's possession soon after the theft, either theft or reset may be inferred. The difficulty is in defining "recent". In the case of *MacLennan* v *MacKenzie* (1987), 2½ months was too long for theft but not too long for reset. In *L* v *Wilson* (1995), 7 days was too long for robbery, but, again, not too long for reset.

Wilful blindness

The courts have accepted a form of wilful blindness to be equivalent to knowledge. This is an extreme form of blinding oneself to the obvious. Effectively, the court assumes that the accused has already formed the conclusion that the goods were stolen and that this constitutes the only reason that he did not specifically ask.

The leading case is *Latta* v *Herron* (1967). A solicitor who was building up a collection of weapons as a hobby was charged with reset. He had bought guns from one of his clients. The two guns were collectors' items and the solicitor had collected them from the client when he met him in a close or alleyway, late at night, paying about half of their actual value. He was convicted of reset and, on appeal, the High Court affirmed the sheriff's view that the solicitor had wilfully blinded himself to the obvious. If he did not know the firearms were stolen when he bought them, it must have been obvious shortly afterwards.

EMBEZZLEMENT

It can be difficult to distinguish between theft and embezzlement. Embezzlement is the intentional, dishonest appropriation of property which the owner has entrusted to the accused (or with which the accused has been authorised, by the owner, to deal), to the accused's own purposes (which are outwith the scope of the authorisation) such that the accused fails to account to the owner for the property.

Actus reus

There are several strands to the *actus reus*:

(1) the accused must hold the property with the victim's consent;

(2) the accused must have the power to administer the property and a corresponding duty to account for those dealings;

(3) the accused must have commenced dealing with the property as authorised. In *Guild* v *Lees* (1994), the secretary of the World Curling Federation drew a cheque on an account which he was

authorised to use when travelling abroad. He used the proceeds to pay his domestic electricity bill. The High Court said that this *did* constitute embezzlement because he was using the money for an unauthorised purpose. So, the fact that the money came from that particular account was not important but rather the fact that he drew the money in the course of generally administering the club's account;

(4) the accused must have failed to account to the victim for the property.

Mens rea

The *mens rea* of embezzlement is a dishonest intention to appropriate the victim's property to the accused's own use. The accused's intention to pay the money back is irrelevant. In *Allenby* v *HM Advocate* (1938), the accused was an agent for fishermen. He advanced money from a bank account to fishermen who were *not* entitled to it, but he did this openly. Because he had not tried to conceal his actions, it was not clear that his intention was dishonest – nor had the jury been told that it needed to be. His conviction for embezzlement was quashed.

FRAUD

Macdonald defines fraud as "the bringing about of any practical result by false pretences" (52) but this is only a statement of the *actus reus*.

Fraud is the bringing about of any practical result by a false pretence where the accused is aware of the falsity of the pretence and has the intention of using it to bring about the practical result. The victim must have been deceived by the false pretence and have acted on the basis of it.

Actus reus

There are three elements to the *actus reus* of fraud:

(1) The false pretence

The false pretence may be express or implied. An omission is sufficient if there is a duty to make a representation.

In *James Paton* (1858), bulls entered in a livestock competition were made to look better by having air pumped under their skin and their horns falsely lengthened. This was held to amount to an implied representation that the bulls really were bigger.

(2) The practical result

The recipient of the false pretence must actually be deceived by it. Almost any practical result of the deception will be sufficient to constitute fraud. For example, in *William Fraser* (1847), persuading a woman to have sexual intercourse by pretending to be her husband was held to be a type of fraud.

In *Adcock* v *Archibald* (1925), a miner attached a tag which identified a colleague's pile of coal as his. The only practical result was that his employers recorded him as having dug more coal than in fact he had. He did not receive any more money as a result. This was sufficient to constitute a practical result.

(3) Causal link

The practical result must be caused by the false pretence. If the person's actions would have been the same, even if there were no false pretence, then the crime of fraud has not been committed.

Mens rea

The *mens rea* of fraud requires the accused to be aware of the falseness of the representation and to intend to bring about the practical result.

UTTERING

Uttering is the Scottish form of forgery and is so called because it is not enough simply to forge a document – it must actually be "uttered as genuine", in the sense of being issued or otherwise put beyond the control of the accused – before any crime is constituted.

Uttering is exposing a forgery to another person as genuine in the knowledge that it is forged and with the intention that he or she should be deceived by it.

Actus reus

The *actus reus* consists in exposing a forged document to another person as if it were genuine. It is not necessary that the accused made the forgery himself; exposing it is sufficient. There is no need to establish a practical result.

What is a forgery?

In the case of *Simon Fraser* (1859), it was held that a document is only a forgery where the document is "intended to represent and pass for the genuine writing of another person" (at 475). Where, as here, the accused, with the help of a colleague, created and signed a document which contained completely false information, this was not uttering. The accused and his colleague still represented themselves as themselves.

Exposing to another person as genuine

The forged document may be "uttered" as genuine by, for example, being presented to a third party, being presented to the public at large or simply by being put beyond the accused's control in some way, perhaps by posting it.

Mens rea

The *mens rea* of uttering requires the Crown to prove that the accused *knew* that the document was false *and* that he or she intended the other party to be deceived by it.

ROBBERY

Robbery consists in theft accomplished by means of personal violence or the threat of violence, where the accused overcomes the victim's will to obtain the property. Although robbery always involves a theft, theft and robbery are distinct crimes.

Actus reus

The *actus reus* requires:

(1) Theft

The *actus reus* of robbery requires theft (where the appropriation is accomplished simply by taking the property from its owner or possessor there and then) brought about by violence. It is not necessary that the victim should actually own the property – merely that it is in his care.

(2) Violence

The violence must be applied either immediately before, or at the same time as, the taking of the property. Assaulting someone *after* taking their property is not robbery.

"Against his will". The victim's will can be overcome by intimidation without the accused ever using actual violence against him. In such a case, the Crown must establish that the will was completely overcome. In *Harrison* v *Jessop* (1992), two employees were told that they would not be allowed to leave their employer's premises unless the contents of the till were handed over to an agent of an alleged creditor of the employer's. It was established that the money had been handed over against the employees' wills. The accused's conviction for robbery was upheld on appeal.

Provided that there is sufficient evidence of some violence, robbery can be constituted even where the violence used does not amount to an assault in its own right: *O'Neill* v *HM Advocate* (1934).

Mens rea

It appears that the *mens rea* of theft is required but accompanied by the intention to use the violence to obtain the goods.

EXTORTION

Extortion consists in obtaining money, property or any other advantage by threats. In the case of *Black* v *Carmichael* (1992), wheel-clamping, carried out by a private company, was held to amount to extortion. The court decided that private wheel-clamping expresses the essence of extortion. The owner of the car was faced with the "threat" that it would not be released from the clamp unless he paid a sum of money to the wheel-clampers.

It is not necessary that the advantage which the accused seeks to obtain should be the payment of money. For example, in *Rae* v *Donnelly* (1982), the accused threatened to disclose that two of his employees had been having an affair, unless one of them dropped a claim for wrongful dismissal. This was held to amount to extortion.

Essential Facts

- Theft can be committed only against corporeal, moveable property which is in the ownership of someone else.
- Information is incorporeal, therefore it cannot be stolen. Only the paper or memory stick containing the information can be taken.

- The *actus reus* of theft is appropriation. It may also be constituted by *amotio* – moving the object in such a way that the intention to steal can be inferred – and by the retention of found property.

- The *mens rea* of theft is intentionally depriving the owner of his or her property permanently, indefinitely or temporarily.

- If the *mens rea* is temporary deprivation, it appears that the taking of the goods must be clandestine, for a nefarious purpose and that the case itself must be exceptional: *Milne* v *Tudhope* (1981). Subsequent cases have not always applied these requirements, treating the intention to deprive temporarily as sufficient in itself: *Black* v *Carmichael* (1992).

- Housebreaking, an aggravation of theft, is committed by over-coming the security of any shut and fast, roofed building. The housebreaking must precede the theft, or be the means by which it is achieved.

- Theft by opening lockfast places, another aggravation, consists in breaking into anything secured by a lock, other than a house, such as a car, a jewellery box or a room within a building.

- Section 57 of the Civic Government (Scotland) Act 1982 makes it an offence for anyone to be found on premises in circumstances from which an intent to commit theft can reasonably be inferred.

- Section 58 of the 1982 Act makes it an offence for anyone with two or more previous convictions for theft to be found in possession of tools from which an intention to commit theft can reasonably be inferred.

- The *actus reus* of reset is the retention of goods which have been obtained dishonestly. Conniving at such possession can also constitute the necessary criminal behaviour.

- The *mens rea* is the knowledge that the goods are stolen and the intention to deprive the owner of them.

- The doctrine of recent possession allows the court to infer that the accused is guilty of reset, or theft, or robbery, if he is found in possession of goods which have been misappropriated shortly after the alleged crime of dishonesty took place. A longer period is allowed for reset than for theft or robbery.

- The doctrine of wilful blindness allows the court to infer that the accused has deliberately not tried to ascertain if the relevant goods are stolen, because she must, in all the circumstances, have reached the conclusion that they were. This is treated as the equivalent of knowledge for establishing the *mens rea* of reset.

• Embezzlement arises where the owner has entrusted property to the accused which he has then misappropriated so that he cannot account to the owner for his dealings with it.

• The accused must have started dealing with the property as authorised.

• The *mens rea* is the dishonest intention to appropriate the property to the accused's own use.

• The *actus reus* of fraud is a false pretence which brings about a practical result. The victim must actually have been deceived by the falsity and have acted upon it.

• The *mens rea* is the awareness that the pretence is false and the intention to deceive the victim by it.

• Uttering requires the accused to "utter" (by, for example, showing it to a third party or posting it) a forgery (a writing purporting to be the writing of another person) as genuine.

• The *mens rea* is the knowledge that the forgery is false and the intention to deceive the victim by it.

• Robbery is theft accomplished by personal violence or the threat thereof. The violence must precede the theft or be the means of achieving it.

• The *mens rea* of robbery requires that the accused should intend to deprive the victim of the property by the use of violence.

• Extortion is obtaining any advantage by threats.

Essential Cases

Dewar (1777): breaking into the accused's employer's premises and copying out trade secrets did not amount to theft by housebreaking.

HM Advocate v Mackenzies (1913): making copies of secret trade recipes with the intention of selling them did not amount to theft.

Grant v Allan (1987): dishonest exploitation of confidential information is not a crime known to the law of Scotland.

Dewar v HM Advocate (1945): appropriation in theft takes place at the moment when the accused forms the intention to deprive the owner of the goods. This will be inferred from the surrounding circumstances.

Kivlin v Milne (1979): intention to deprive the owner permanently of his property may be inferred from the abandonment of that property where he or she is unlikely to find it.

Milne v Tudhope (1981): intention to deprive the owner of his or her property only temporarily is enough to constitute the *mens rea* of theft but only in exceptional cases where the taking is clandestine and for a nefarious purpose.

Black v Carmichael (1992): the practice of private wheel-clamping may amount to both theft and extortion. The property is appropriated at the moment when the wheel clamp is applied and the owner is deprived of the possession and use of the vehicle. Accordingly, deprivation of any of the rights of ownership is sufficient to constitute theft; there is no need for the property to be physically removed.

Fowler v O'Brien (1994): intention to deprive the owner of his property indefinitely is sufficient to constitute the *mens rea* of theft.

HM Advocate v Forbes (1994): housebreaking is only a criminal offence when accompanied by theft or the intention to steal. The intention to commit another crime (here, rape) is insufficient.

Latta v Herron (1967): wilful blindness to the fact that goods have obviously been obtained dishonestly can be treated as the knowledge required to establish the *mens rea* of reset.

Simon Fraser (1859): a document is only a forgery for the purposes of uttering if it purports to be the writing of another person.

5 ART AND PART LIABILITY

Art and part liability is also sometimes referred to as "aiding and abetting", "acting along with" and "acting in concert". It allows others, in addition to the actual perpetrator(s) of a crime, to be convicted because of their involvement in the overall criminal enterprise. Sometimes, this involvement can be established because their actings prior to committing the crime demonstrate that they have entered into a common plan to carry out the criminal offence. In other cases, participation in the crime itself is enough to establish criminal liability.

According to Lord Justice-General Cullen in *McKinnon* v *HM Advocate* (2003):

> "[i]t is, of course, well established that, where a number of persons act together in pursuance of a common criminal purpose, each of them is criminally responsible for a crime which is committed in pursuance of that purpose, regardless of the part which he or she played, provided that the crime is within the scope of that common criminal purpose. This holds good whether the concert is antecedent or spontaneous" (at 39).

Thus, the lookout and the getaway driver can be found guilty of a bank robbery in exactly the same way as those who actually enter the building and take the money.

BEING PRESENT DURING THE COMMISSION OF A CRIME

Observing

It is not enough that an accused happens to be present when a crime is committed and to observe it taking place.

This point is made in *Geo Kerr and Others* (1871), where one accused watched through the hedge from the next field as the other two assaulted the victim. He was acquitted.

Being present and apparently profiting

In *Lawler* v *Neizer* (1993), the accused was found with 54 £1 notes in his possession. These had been passed to him by a co-accused who had bought a round of drinks with a counterfeit bank note. The co-accused wanted to have less money on his person when he himself was searched. The accused was convicted at first instance. On appeal, the High Court quashed the conviction, on the basis that being present at the scene of the crime, even when coupled with possession of the money, was not sufficient to establish art and part guilt.

FORMS OF ART AND PART LIABILITY

Art and part liability may be established in any of four ways:

(1) Common plan (or "by counsel")

To establish art and part liability generally, the prosecution must prove that there was a "common criminal purpose" among the co-accused. Where this purpose is pre-arranged, so that the accused organise and agree the criminal activity in advance, it is referred to as a "common plan".

If there is no common plan or purpose, each accused is judged on his own actions. This is illustrated by the case of *Johnston* v *HM Advocate* (2009). In this case, two accused were convicted of the murder of the victim even though the jury determined that each had acted separately and individually and not "in concert" with one another. One had "knocked the deceased to the floor and then delivered eight powerful punches to his head" (para 29, per Lord Reed) rendering him unconscious. The second accused had then kicked the victim's head, "as if he were taking a penalty kick with a football." (para 29, per Lord Reed) It was impossible to determine which blow was the cause of death. Each accused was separately convicted of murder, on the basis of his own acts. The court specifically did *not* find that they had acted in concert. If, on the other hand, the prosecution can prove the existence of a common plan, it will be able to obtain art and part convictions for all of those who were parties to that plan.

The leading case on art and part liability (a five-judge decision of the High Court) affirms the importance of the common plan as the measure of the liability of the co-accused. In *McKinnon* v *HM Advocate* (2003) four co-accused had been together in the house of one of them and had formulated a plan to go to the victims' house to commit robbery. One of the co-accused agreed to go and obtain, from his father-in-law, a set of chef's knives. On arrival at the victims' property, the co-accused broke down the close door and attacked the occupants of the victims' flat. Two of the victims were injured and the third, who had been stabbed three times in the chest, died. The forensic evidence indicated that only one person had inflicted the fatal blows. All four were, however, convicted of both the assaults and the murder, on the basis of art and part liability.

The appeal was referred to a Full Bench of the High Court in order to obtain an authoritative ruling on the principles of art and part liability. The court held that an objective approach was appropriate. This would determine which crime had been committed (here, murder) and would then hold all accused who had been parties to the common plan responsible for that murder. This was on the basis that, because the accused had gone in the knowledge that the knives might be used to facilitate the robbery, it should have been clear to all of them, following from the common plan, that there was an obvious risk of taking life. Unless there was any question of the common plan having been exceeded, it was not appropriate to approach the matter subjectively and to try to determine the mindset of each individual accused towards the crime. If the Crown could establish a common plan, in terms of which there arose such an obvious risk of taking life, each accused was automatically responsible for the crime by virtue of entering into that plan in the first place.

It was clarified in *Poole* v *Advocate* (2009) that this effectively means that a different form of mental element is to be applied in art and part murder cases. Lord Kingarth stated:

> "The question, following *McKinnon* v *HM Advocate*, comes to be whether there was evidence entitling the jury to find that it was objectively foreseeable to the appellant that such violence was liable to be used as carried an obvious risk of life being taken. The question is not … whether there was evidence from which it could be said that the appellant had the mens rea necessary for murder (para 11)."

(2) By instigation

"Instigation" occurs where another person is procured to commit a crime. One of the clearest examples of this form of art and part liability is the hiring of a contract killer. Both the perpetrator and the person who hired him or her will be guilty, art and part, of the eventual crime. This form of art and part liability is touched on in *HM Advocate* v *Meikleham and Parker* (1998).

On the other hand, simple advice is not enough to constitute art and part liability. There must be some evidence of actual involvement in the planning and/or commission of the crime.

In *Martin* v *Hamilton* (1989), the accused was charged with advising another person to commit an offence. The accused was a solicitor. A client told him that he had earlier been involved in a car accident but had not reported it to the police. The solicitor was charged with allegedly advising the client not to report the offence, and thus impliedly advising him to commit an offence. Because it appeared that the offence had already been committed by the time the client consulted the solicitor, the solicitor could not be convicted of aiding and abetting its commission. Art and part liability cannot arise *after* the commission of the offence.

(3) By provision of material assistance

The third way of establishing art and part liability is by the provision of material assistance in the commission of the crime. For this to be established, the accused must have knowledge of the criminal plot. Second, the assistance given must have a real connection with the actual crime in contemplation. Finally, the commission of the crime must be imminent.

In the case of *HM Advocate* v *Johnstone and Stewart* (1926) the accused, Johnstone, was indicted because she had supplied Stewart's name as someone who would carry out a backstreet abortion. Johnstone did not know Stewart and had received no financial benefit for providing the information. It was held, because of the absence of any real connection between Johnstone and Stewart, that art and part liability could not be established.

(4) By taking part in the commission of the crime

The fourth way in which someone can be held to be guilty, art and part, of a criminal offence is where he took part in its commission. The Crown must prove the existence of a "common criminal purpose". In *Gallacher* v *HM Advocate* (1951), the Mills Brothers' circus was visiting Hamilton. A crowd of people, with an unexplained grudge against the circus personnel, arrived as the Big Top was being dismantled. A group of about six or seven were seen by a number of witnesses kicking a man, who had no connection with the circus, while he lay on the ground. He subsequently died from his injuries. Three members of the group were arrested by the police at the scene. All were convicted of murder and sentenced to death, on the basis that they had been acting in concert.

In the case of *Bonar and Hogg* v *McLeod* (1983), the accused were police officers who were convicted of assaulting a prisoner, by grasping his throat, and by twisting his arm up his back while "fast-marching" him along a passage in the police station. Only one of the officers (the more junior) had actually inflicted the injury. The second officer was found guilty art and part. The common purpose arose from the senior officer assisting his colleague in taking the prisoner along the passage and also from his seniority, in that he had not intervened to stop the assault.

AVOIDING ART AND PART LIABILITY

Withdrawal from the common plan

If the crime is still at the planning stage, it appears that the accused can withdraw and escape liability for the completed offence. This is on the basis that he will not actually have participated in perpetration of the crime. For successful withdrawal, it may also be necessary to prove that the intention to withdraw had been clearly indicated to the co-accused prior to the perpetration stage *and* that the withdrawer had tried to discourage the co-accused from going ahead.

Where perpetration of the crime has actually commenced, however, it is impossible for an accused to withdraw. In *MacNeil* v *HM Advocate* (1986) one of the six co-accused, Christopher Socratous, appealed against his conviction for importing cannabis into the UK. He had been employed as an engineer on a ship and had helped to store a cargo of cannabis in a fuel tank. He claimed that he had done this merely to ensure that the cargo was safely stored and that he had left the ship at the first possible opportunity after the cargo of drugs was loaded. By doing so, he argued that he had completely dissociated himself from the criminal enterprise and that his conviction should be overturned. In the appeal, the High Court held that there is no defence of dissociation from a criminal enterprise which has commenced.

It does not appear that the point about actively taking steps to prevent the commission of the crime has been tested in any other case. However, it is very likely that it would involve, at a minimum, contacting the relevant authorities.

Unintended consequences

Art and part liability makes all accused who shared the common criminal purpose responsible for all consequences of their common actions. It does not matter how small a part in the actual commission each, as an individual, has actually played. If a co-accused can prove that he did not fully share the common criminal purpose, however, he will be judged only on his own actions.

Pre-concert: going beyond the common plan

Where there has been pre-concert, there may be occasions where the actions of an individual accused go beyond the previously agreed common plan. In that instance, the co-accused will escape liability for those additional actions which they could not have foreseen.

In *Boyne* v *HM Advocate* (1980), Boyne and his co-accused Brown were found guilty, art and part, of murder by stabbing. The fatal blows had actually been inflicted by a third accused named Curley. There was, however, no evidence that either Boyne or Brown knew or should have foreseen that Curley would use a knife in the course of the attack. Because this action went beyond the common plan, Boyne's and Brown's murder convictions were quashed. A conviction for assault and robbery was substituted in both cases.

In *Hopkinson* v *HM Advocate* (2009), the victim had been stabbed to death in the course of a robbery. Both co-accused were convicted of murder at first instance. The second co-accused had himself gone armed with a knife but with the intention only of threatening the victim if he refused to hand over his money. His evidence was that he had not known until he was on his way to the locus that his co-accused had a knife and he had no reason to anticipate that she would use it to stab the victim, let alone in such a way as to cause his death. He was initially convicted of murder on an art and part basis but his appeal was successful. It should have been left to the jury to consider whether the common criminal purpose included the taking of life or the material risk of life being taken. If it did not then the co-accused had gone beyond the common plan. Her actions were not foreseeable in its terms. The fact that Hopkinson had himself gone armed with a knife was not conclusive. It was the purpose for which he thought it would be used which was important.

No pre-concert

Where there has been no pre-concert, and the criminality arises spontaneously, the responsibility of each co-accused is determined by their overall knowledge of the situation and the foreseeability of the eventual outcome.

Early participation only. In *Codona* v *HM Advocate* (1996), the accused, aged 14, had gone to Queen's Park in Glasgow with a group of young men whose purpose was to assault others whom they believed to be homosexual. The group had already assaulted two men that evening. The third assault was more vicious and the victim died as a result of repeated kicking and stamping on his head and neck. Claire Codona was initially convicted of murder, art and part, on the basis that she had been part of the gang which was responsible for the killing and that she had kicked the deceased once, on the back of the legs, at an early stage in the assault.

On appeal, her conviction was quashed. The court took the view that, given that the two previous attacks had resulted in relatively minor injuries to the victims, it would not have been foreseeable to her that this attack would escalate into a fatal one. Thus, participation in an assault at an early stage will not necessarily give rise to art and part guilt of homicide if it could not have been foreseen that the assault would be fatal.

Latecoming. By the same token, a latecomer who is unaware of the earlier (fatal) attacks may not be implicated in the murder. In *Kabalu* v *HM Advocate* (1999), the accused arrived at the end of a murderous assault and delivered one or two kicks or stamps to the victim's head. It was held that, since he had not seen the serious violence which preceded his arrival, he could not be held to be acting in concert in relation to the murderous violence. Since this was the only way in which he could be found guilty of murder – his own actions not amounting to a murderous attack in themselves – his conviction for murder was quashed and a conviction for assault substituted.

Homicide cases. In art and part homicide cases, where there *is* pre-concert and the common plan is such that it was objectively foreseeable to the co-accused that the violence liable to be used was such as to carry an obvious risk of life being taken, each co-accused will be guilty of murder. This is the effect of *McKinnon* v *HM Advocate* (2003) and *Poole* v *HM Advocate* (2009). Where there is no pre-concert, however – ie in circumstances where the common purpose to commit the crime arises spontaneously – it remains possible, in homicide cases, for one co-accused to be convicted of murder and another of culpable homicide. In *Docherty* v *HM Advocate* (2003), it was unclear which of two co-accused had inflicted the fatal stab wound but there was evidence that one of them had taken the lead in the criminal enterprise. He had attracted the victim's attention, struck the first blow (to the head with the knife) and had laughed when a witness subsequently asked about the murder. The court held that it was appropriate to convict him of murder and his co-accused of culpable homicide.

Effect of acquittal of principal offender

Finally, there is the issue of the effect of the acquittal of the principal offender(s) on a co-accused, whose involvement in the criminal enterprise can be proved only on an art and part basis. This depends very much on the nature of the criminal conduct charged. In most cases, it is possible to convict an accessory even if the principal offender is acquitted, as in *Capuano* v *HM Advocate* (1985) where the charge was being part of a group which had carried out an assault by throwing bricks and stones at a car.

Where the charge is more specialised, so that only the holder of a particular office could be convicted of it, then, if all such officer-bearers are acquitted, it appears that art and part liability cannot attach to anyone else. Thus, in *Young and Todd* v *HM Advocate* (1932), Young, who was not a director or company secretary of a particular company, was acquitted of a charge which could only be committed by individuals holding one of those posts. They had all been acquitted previously.

Essential Facts

- Art and part liability allows persons other than those who physically committed the offence to be convicted, because of their involvement in the overall criminal enterprise.
- The Crown must prove that a common criminal purpose existed among the co-accused.
- Merely observing a crime taking place is insufficient, in itself, to incur art and part liability.
- Art and part liability may be established by the pre-existence of a common plan setting out how the crime is to be committed. In that event, all parties to the common plan are liable for the completed offence.
- The mental element in art and part murder cases where there is pre-concert (ie a pre-existing common plan) is established if it was objectively foreseeable to the co-accused that such violence was liable to be used as carried an obvious risk of life being taken. It is *not* whether each co-accused individually had the *mens rea* for murder.
- Where there is no pre-concert (where the accused came together spontaneously), the court will consider the actions and mindset of

each accused separately so that one may be convicted of murder and another of culpable homicide.

- In addition to the "common plan" scenario, art and part liability may be established by instigation (where the accused procures another person to commit the crime), by providing material assistance with, or by taking part in, its commission.

- It is impossible to withdraw from the common plan after perpetration of the crime has commenced. Withdrawal at the preparation stage may be possible if the accused tried to prevent his co-accused from proceeding any further.

- Where an accused goes beyond the common plan, his co-accused will not be liable for the excessive act(s) if those acts were unforeseeable.

- Where there is no pre-concert, an accused must be judged by the state of his knowledge of the circumstances of the crime.

- Where the principal offender is acquitted, it may still be possible to find a co-accused guilty on an art and part basis, depending on the nature of the crime.

Essential Cases

Geo Kerr and Others (1871): merely observing a crime is not sufficient to establish art and part liability.

McKinnon v HM Advocate (2003): where there is a common plan, the responsibility of the co-accused is judged objectively. The court first determines which crime has been committed. It then finds all co-accused who were parties to the common plan guilty of that. The matter turns on whether or not the common plan gives rise to an obvious risk of a particular outcome. In homicide cases, if there is an obvious risk of taking life, the crime is murder.

Poole v HM Advocate (2009): the mental element in art and part murder cases where there is pre-concert is whether or not it was objectively foreseeable to a co-accused that such violence was liable to be used as carried an obvious risk of life being taken.

Gallacher v HM Advocate (1951): anyone who shares the common criminal purpose and participates in the commission of the crime is guilty of the crime, no matter how minor his role.

MacNeil v HM Advocate (1986): it is impossible to escape criminal liability by withdrawing from the common plan once perpetration of the crime has commenced.

Boyne v HM Advocate (1980): where an accused goes beyond the terms of the common plan, his co-accused will not be guilty of the excess provided that his actions were unforeseeable to them.

Hopkinson v HM Advocate (2009): in a murder case, even where a co-accused (who did not inflict the fatal blow) goes to the locus armed with a potentially lethal weapon, it must still be left to the jury to consider whether the common criminal purpose included the taking of life or the material risk of life being taken. If it did not, the common plan has been exceeded and that co-accused will not be guilty of murder on an art and part basis.

Codona v HM Advocate (1996): participation at the outset of an attack only, when the accused could not have known that the violence would escalate, is insufficient to establish art and part liability for the fatal consequences of a spontaneous attack.

Kabalu v HM Advocate (1999): attacking a victim after a murderous attack has been carried out is not sufficient to make a co-accused art and part liable for the murder if he could not have known that such violence had previously been used.

Docherty v HM Advocate (2003): in a homicide case, where there is no pre-concert, the responsibility of each accused may be assessed separately, allowing them to be found guilty of different crimes.

Capuano v HM Advocate (1985): an accessory may be found guilty of the crime charged even if the principal offender is acquitted.

6 INCHOATE CRIME

The area of inchoate crime deals with offences which are started but not completed. In certain circumstances – classified as attempt, conspiracy and incitement – such behaviour is also criminalised.

CRIMINAL ATTEMPTS

In general, the attempt to commit a crime is as criminal as the completed act.

Attempts to commit crime are specifically made criminal in their own right by s 294 of the Criminal Procedure (Scotland) Act 1995.

Actus reus

The criminal law does not punish a mere intention to commit a crime. Some conduct is also necessary. The difficulty is deciding what conduct will suffice. The law requires some positive action on the part of the accused before it will hold them responsible for the attempted crime.

"Preparation to perpetration" test

The most commonly used test is the "preparation to perpetration" test. In other words, the court asks whether it can draw the inference that the accused has moved from the preparation stage, towards actual commission of the crime, by carrying out a positive act or acts.

Although this test is easily stated in words, it can be difficult to apply in practice. As the High Court noted in *Coventry* v *Douglas* (1944) "[t]he line of demarcation between preparation and perpetration cannot be defined in any general proposition" (per Lord Justice-General Normand at 20).

In *HM Advocate* v *Mackenzies* (1913), the accused had "borrowed" a book of chemical formulae and had copied it out. In *Morton* v *Henderson* (1956), the accused had gone round to see the owners of a racing greyhound named Nifty to try to persuade them to drug it so that it would lose a race. In both of these cases, then, the accused had actually done *something* more than just thinking criminal thoughts. In *Mackenzies* he had copied out the chemical formulae and, in *Morton* v *Henderson*, they had gone round to see the greyhound's owners. In neither case was the charge of attempt established, however, because in neither case were the courts prepared to hold that the accused had passed the preparation stage.

Other cases do suggest that any step beyond preparation will be sufficient. In *HM Advocate* v *Camerons* (1911), the accused were convicted of attempting to defraud an insurance company. They had faked a robbery but had not actually got as far as presenting the insurance claim when they were apprehended. Nonetheless, the robbery, and the fact that they had communicated that it had happened to the insurance company, were positive steps towards the perpetration of the fraud and this was enough to establish the attempt.

In *Barrett* v *Allan* (1986), the accused was convicted of attempting to enter a football ground while drunk – a statutory offence. He had twice joined the queue at the turnstile while drunk, the second time after being warned by the police not to do so. The case discusses a number of possible interpretations of the shift to perpetration. The match was in Edinburgh. The sheriff rejects the idea that if the accused, who lived in Glasgow, had only got as far as Queen Street Station in Glasgow, that would have been enough to constitute the criminal attempt – even though it is a positive act towards entering an Edinburgh football ground. Equally, the defence argument that you could only attempt to enter a football ground when actually going through the turnstile was rejected as requiring too much. The commentary on the case takes the common-sense view that "to join a queue in order to enter a place is an attempt to enter it" (at 481).

"Final stage" test

It is fairly well accepted today that whether an attempt is criminal rests on the "preparation to perpetration" test. However, other tests have been applied on occasion, and it is important to be aware of these. They can be encapsulated under the heading of "final stage" test, and they break down into two categories:

(a) **"Last act" theory.** This theory takes the view that the accused is guilty of an attempt to commit a crime where he or she has done everything necessary to commit that crime. In *Janet Ramage* (1825), the accused had put poison in a teapot from which the intended victim was expected to drink some tea. This was the "last act" necessary to commit the crime. After that, all that could be done was to wait to see if the expected consequence (the victim's death) did indeed ensue.

Similarly, in *Samuel Tumbelson* (1863), the accused had poisoned some oatmeal with strychnine and had given it to another member of his household, with strict instructions that she should ensure that his wife ate it. Again, he had done everything he could to commit the crime of murder. The fact that his wife had not eaten the oatmeal did not affect the status of his original action as a criminal offence.

(b) "Irrevocability" theory. This is the most extreme test of all. It requires that the accused has done so much towards committing the crime that it is no longer possible for him or her to intervene to prevent its commission. In modern Scots law, this theory appears to rest on a statement by Lord Wark in *HM Advocate* v *Tannahill and Neilson* (1943) that, in order to constitute a criminal attempt, there has to be "some overt act, the consequences of which cannot be recalled by the accused" (at 153).

This approach is implicit in at least one more recent case. In *McKenzie* v *HM Advocate* (1988), the accused had formed a fraudulent scheme to obtain money from a company named Caley Fisheries (Partnerships) Ltd. Part of this scheme involved persuading a firm of solicitors to raise actions against Caley for money which was not due. Much of the argument in the case turned on whether the raising of a court action was or was not irrevocable.

Mens rea

The mental element in all criminal attempts is the same as for the completed crime. This was affirmed in *Cawthorne* v *HM Advocate* (1968) which held that the *mens rea* for attempted murder is the same as for murder itself. Here, the accused had fired a shotgun with wicked recklessness as to the consequences (one possible *mens rea* of murder). His conviction for attempted murder was upheld on appeal.

Attempting to do the impossible

Much legal and philosophical commentary has been devoted to the issue of the appropriate response to someone who attempts to do the impossible. This situation can arise in two ways.

Legal impossibility

First, the individual may be mistaken in his belief that the act undertaken, even if completed, constitutes a criminal offence. If it does not, then he can never be guilty of it as a criminal offence

Factual impossibility

The other possibility is that the individual embarks on a course of conduct which he or she believes to constitute a criminal offence but that, due to some fact of which they are, at the time, unaware, it would be impossible ever to commit the completed crime. The case of *Docherty* v *Brown* (1996) resolved the difficulties in such cases.

There, the charge was attempting to possess drugs with intent to supply, contrary to ss 5(3) and 19 of the Misuse of Drugs Act 1971. The accused had obtained some tablets in the belief that they contained a controlled substance, when in fact they did not. Because of this, it would have been impossible to convict him of the completed offence. At no time was he actually in possession of controlled drugs contrary to the 1971 Act. The five-judge High Court held that the attempt to commit a crime was a distinct offence from the completed crime itself. Accordingly, if the accused had the *mens rea* for the completed crime and had taken some positive step to bring it about, he could be convicted of the attempt regardless of the impossibility of conviction for the completed offence. Here, the fact that Docherty had fully intended to obtain possession of a controlled substance – and had moved from preparation to perpetration by getting hold of what he thought was the relevant substance – was enough to satisfy both of the limbs of the test of a criminal attempt.

CONSPIRACY

Conspiracy is an inchoate crime involving more than one person. The *mens rea* is intention (to agree to commit a crime) and the *actus reus* is entering into that agreement. The two elements are, therefore, virtually indistinguishable from each other.

The definition of conspiracy in the criminal law is usually taken from the civil case of *Crofter Hand Woven Harris Tweed Co* v *Veitch* (1942):

> "Conspiracy, when regarded as a crime, is the agreement of two or more persons to effect any unlawful purpose, whether as their ultimate aim, or only as a means to it, and the crime is complete if there is such agreement, even though nothing is done in pursuance of it" (per Lord Chancellor Viscount Simon at 5).

Thus, the accused must agree to do something which would, if it were actually carried out, constitute a criminal offence under Scots law. It does not matter whether it is the actual end purpose of the agreement which is criminal or merely one of the means to achieving it.

No conduct necessary

The crime of conspiracy is complete at the moment when the accused agree to achieve a criminal purpose. There is no need to establish any step from preparation to perpetration. There may, however, be a difficulty with proving the conspiracy, if no action has been taken in furtherance of the agreement. In *Carberry* v *HM Advocate* (1975), the accused were charged with conspiracy to commit assault and robbery in a bank. The crime would have been complete as soon as they agreed with each other to do this. In fact, at first instance, the jury were instructed that there would not be enough evidence to convict the accused of the conspiracy if they were not satisfied that the accused had been seen observing the bank in a stolen car on each of two consecutive days. The Crown also led evidence about other possible preparations which they had actually made (including keeping gloves and stocking masks in the stolen car).

Conspiracy as a continuing crime

As a crime, conspiracy does not come to an end as soon as the relevant agreement has been reached. It continues until either the criminal purpose is achieved or the agreement is abandoned. This means that a number of accused may be convicted of the conspiracy even if each became a party to the agreement at a different time.

Conspiracies with a foreign element

It is not appropriate to leave the discussion of the Scots law on conspiracy without briefly mentioning the proceedings arising out of the bombing of PanAm Flight 103 over Lockerbie on 21 December 1988 (*HM Advocate* v *Al-Megrahi* (2000)). One of the charges in the original case, against both accused, was conspiracy, *inter alia*, to destroy an aircraft and to murder its occupants. The issue was whether the Scottish courts had jurisdiction over a conspiracy which had not taken place in Scotland. The court held that the fact that the completed crime had taken place in Scotland gave it jurisdiction over the conspiracy.

It is also implicit in the judgment that, if accused conspire to commit a crime in Scotland, that is sufficient to give the Scottish courts jurisdiction, even if no concrete acts to fulfil the conspiracy actually take place on Scottish soil.

INCITEMENT

Incitement is an attempt to form a conspiracy and therefore criminalises behaviour at a very early stage. In *Morton* v *Henderson* (1956), the accuseds' actions in calling on Nifty the greyhound's owners and asking them to participate in the betting scam would have been enough to amount to incitement. It was never so charged, however.

It is possible to obtain a conviction for incitement even where there is no clear instruction from the accused to the other person actually to carry out the crime. This is important in relation to "contract killings". In *Baxter* v *HM Advocate* (1998), the accused held a conversation, under the Forth Bridge, with a man named Ingle, about the desirability of killing a third party called Gardner. The court held that all that was necessary was that the jury should be satisfied that the accused seriously intended Ingle to kill Gardner. If that was so, it was enough that the accused had encouraged or requested him to do so. There was no need for a specific instruction to kill to be given.

Essential Facts

- Inchoate crime covers offences which are started but not completed.

- In general, the attempt to commit a crime is equally as criminal as the completed offence itself.

- The *mens rea* of a criminal attempt is the *mens rea* for the completed crime. The *actus reus* requires evidence of a positive act towards completion of the crime. This is described as a move from mere preparation to perpetration.

- A criminal attempt is a crime distinct from the completed offence itself. Thus, even if it would be impossible for the accused ever to commit the completed offence, he or she can still be found guilty of the attempt if they hold the *mens rea* of the completed crime and have taken a positive step towards its perpetration.

- Conspiracy must be committed by more than one person. The *actus reus* is entering into an agreement to commit a crime; the *mens rea* is the intention to enter into that agreement.

- It is equally criminal to conspire to use criminal means to bring about an end which may, in itself, be lawful.

- As a crime, conspiracy does not come to an end as soon as the agreement is first reached. It continues until the criminal purpose is achieved or the agreement is abandoned.

- Incitement is the attempt to form a conspiracy. It only needs to be clear that the accused encouraged another to carry out a crime. No specific order to do so is required.

Essential Cases

HM Advocate v Camerons (1911): any positive act towards the completion of the crime which is carried out with the relevant *mens rea* will be sufficient to satisfy the *actus reus* of a criminal attempt.

Barrett v Allan (1986): discussion of the transition from preparation to perpetration.

Cawthorne v HM Advocate (1968): the *mens rea* of a criminal attempt is the same as that of the completed crime.

Docherty v Brown (1996): an accused can be convicted of a criminal attempt even in circumstances where it would be impossible ever to commit the completed crime.

Crofter Hand Woven Harris Tweed Co v Veitch (1942): gives the standard definition of the crime of conspiracy.

HM Advocate v Al-Megrahi (2000): conspiracy is a continuing crime. If the completed crime takes place in Scotland, this gives the Scottish courts jurisdiction over the conspiracy charge.

Baxter v HM Advocate (1998): incitement does not require a specific instruction to carry out the contemplated offence.

7 DEFENCES

SPECIAL DEFENCES

Scots law categorises certain defences as "special" defences. These are alibi, incrimination, self-defence, insanity (at least for the moment), automatism and coercion. Consent is a special defence to certain sex offences in terms of s 6 of the Sexual Offences (Procedure and Evidence) (Scotland) Act 2002. At the time of writing, the special defence available to accused who suffer total alienation of reason, due to mental disorder, disease or disability is the common law defence of insanity. This will be changed by the Criminal Justice and Licensing (Scotland) Bill (hereafter "CJL(S)B") which, once enacted, will place the defence on a statutory basis and rename it "mental disorder". This chapter explains the common law on insanity and discusses the terms of the Bill. Notice of the accused's intention to lead any special defence must be lodged in court prior to the commencement of the trial proceedings (s 78 of the Criminal Procedure (Scotland) Act 1995).

BURDEN OF PROOF

In all cases, it is for the prosecution to prove its case beyond reasonable doubt and the onus of proof remains on the Crown throughout. The only special defence where the onus of proof shifts to the accused is insanity. The accused requires to prove this only on the balance of probabilities. (This will still be the position on onus and burden of proof of the new special defence of mental disorder on enactment of the Bill, which also provides specifically that the accused is the only person who may state it (CJL(S)B s 117 inserting a new s 51A(4) into the Criminal Procedure (Scotland) Act 1995).)

The current, common law, position was established in *Lambie* v *HM Advocate* (1973), where a court of five judges was specially convened to give an authoritative ruling on the issue of onus of proof in special defences generally. (Diminished responsibility, which will be considered in Chapter 10 on Homicide, also operates in this way.)

INSANITY

Insanity is a special defence which, if proved, results in acquittal, although the accused may still be subject to control imposed by the court because of his mental disorder. In addition, or as an alternative, where the accused will be unable to understand the trial process, he may plead insanity in bar of trial. (On enactment, the Bill will change the latter set of provisions so that, if the accused is unable to participate effectively in the trial process, he will be able to plead "unfitness for trial" (CJL(S)B s 119(1), inserting a new s 53F into the Criminal Procedure (Scotland) Act 1995).)

Insanity in bar of trial

The rules on the procedure for a plea of insanity in bar of trial are contained in ss 54–56 of the Criminal Procedure (Scotland) Act 1995. The test, set down in *HM Advocate* v *Wilson* (1942), is whether the accused is fit to instruct a defence and fit to follow the proceedings in court. This may sometimes apply to accused suffering from a physical disability rather than mental disorder. In *Wilson*, for example, the accused was deaf and unable to speak, although the court ultimately determined that he could participate in the trial through an interpreter. In *HM Advocate* v *S* (1999) the accused was a 13-year-old child who suffered from a developmental delay. It was reiterated in *Hughes* v *HM Advocate* (2002) that amnesia does *not* afford a plea in bar of trial. As explained in *Russell* v *HM Advocate* (1946), the important point is to balance fairness to the accused with the public interest in not allowing accused persons to render themselves immune from investigation into their crimes by claiming an incapacity such as amnesia.

On enactment of the Bill the test of unfitness for trial will become statutory: whether or not the accused is "incapable, by reason of a mental or physical condition, of *participating effectively* in a trial" (CJL(S)B, s 119(1), inserting new s 53F(1) of the Criminal Procedure (Scotland) Act 1995). This reflects the standard set, in *T* v *UK; V* v *UK* (2000), by the European Court of Human Rights in relation to the right to a fair trial under Art 6 of the European Convention on Human Rights (1950). In particular, it was held in that case that this standard could not be met merely through representation by "skilled and experienced lawyers" (para 90).

As at common law, the incapability to participate may arise equally from a physical condition as a mental one and amnesia as to the circumstances of the crime cannot, by itself, justify a finding of unfitness to plead (CJL(S)B, s 119(1), inserting new s 53F(3) into the Criminal Procedure (Scotland) Act 1995).

In terms of the Bill, in determining whether the accused is unfit for trial the court is to have regard to:

"the ability of the [accused] to –

- understand the nature of the charge,
- understand the requirement to tender a plea to the charge and the effect of such a plea,
- understand the purpose of, and follow the course of, the trial,
- understand the evidence that may be given against the [accused],
- instruct and otherwise communicate with the [accused's] legal representative, and
- any other factor which the court considers relevant" (CJL(S)B, s 119(1) inserting new s 53F(2) into the Criminal Procedure (Scotland) Act 1995).

The standard of proof of unfitness for trial will be on the balance of probabilities.

To establish the current (common law) plea of insanity in bar of trial, evidence from two medical practitioners is needed. (The CJL(S)B will abolish this requirement.) Their evidence must satisfy the court that the accused is insane so that the trial cannot proceed. If the court is so satisfied, the judge will go on to order an "examination of facts". This takes the place of the trial. It seeks to ascertain whether, in fact, the accused committed the crime and, if so, whether there are any grounds for acquitting him. This procedure will remain in place, following enactment of the Bill, where the accused is found unfit for trial.

Insanity as a special defence

Insanity is a complete defence. If the accused can establish it, he will automatically be acquitted of the crime.

The traditional definition comes from Hume i, 37 where he states that:

"[t]o serve the purpose of a defence in law, the disorder must ... amount to an absolute alienation of reason, ... such a disease as deprives the patient of the knowledge of the true aspect and position of things about him, – hinders him from distinguishing friend or foe, – and gives him up to the impulse of his own distempered fancy."

This definition was adopted in *HM Advocate* v *Kidd* (1960), where a man was accused of the murder of his wife and daughter by administering chloroform to them and then asphyxiating them. He claimed to be suffering from a complete loss of memory as to the events surrounding their deaths. In the course of his charge to the jury, Lord Strachan clarified certain points about insanity as a defence.

First, what he describes as a "mental defect" must have prevented the accused from exercising rational control over his actions. Second, insanity is a purely legal concept. Medical evidence is relevant but it is not the deciding factor. The jury is required to judge the issue as a question of fact taking into account *all* the evidence presented – medical and otherwise – and using their own common sense to determine whether there was an alienation of the reason such that the accused was no longer able to exercise his reason to control his conduct.

The need for alienation of the reason had its most authoritative restatement in the leading case of *Brennan* v *HM Advocate* (1977). The accused was charged with killing his father by stabbing him with a knife. On the day in question he had had somewhere between 20 and 25 pints of beer and a microdot of LSD.

It was held that no one who *voluntarily* consumes alcohol, drugs and/ or other intoxicants, specifically for their intoxicating effect, can then expect to plead insanity if they are subsequently charged with a crime. The special defence of insanity was, therefore, unsuccessful, but the five-judge court did consider the legal definition of insanity which it stated in these terms:

> "In short, insanity in our law requires proof of total alienation of reason in relation to the act charged as the result of mental illness, mental disease or defect or unsoundness of mind and does not comprehend the malfunctioning of the mind of transitory effect, as the result of deliberate and self-induced intoxication. ... The only distinction between insanity and the state of diminished responsibility recognised by our law is that for the latter state to be established something less than total alienation of reason will suffice" (per Lord Justice-General Emslie at 45).

From this, it is clear that insanity requires proof of "*total* alienation of reason". This is a difficult test to meet. If the accused retains *any* correct knowledge and understanding of his or her actions it is arguable that their reason is not *totally* alienated. Second, the alienation of reason must have a direct effect in relation to the act with which the accused is charged. Finally, the alienation must be caused by mental illness, mental disease or defect or unsoundness of mind.

On enactment of the CJL(S)B, the special defence would be renamed "mental disorder" and the test would become that the accused is "unable by reason of mental disorder to appreciate the nature or wrongfulness of the conduct" (CJL(S)B, s 117, inserting new s 51A(1) into the Criminal Procedure (Scotland) Act 1995). Psychopathic personality disorders could not be the basis of a plea of mental disorder though the Bill does not use this term, referring instead to "a personality disorder which is characterised solely or principally by abnormally aggressive or seriously irresponsible conduct" (CJL(S)B, s 117, inserting new s 51A(2) into the Criminal Procedure (Scotland) Act 1995).

Where the accused is acquitted on the ground of mental disorder, the court would be required specifically to declare that this is the case. In solemn proceedings, unless the prosecutor simply accepted the plea, the matter would fall to be determined by the jury (CJL(S)B, s 118, inserting new s 53E into the Criminal Procedure (Scotland) Act 1995).

Disposals

The Criminal Procedure (Scotland) Act 1995, s 57 sets down six possible disposals where the accused is found to be insane, either in bar of trial or by application of the special defence. The same disposals would be available, on enactment of the CJL(S)B where the special defence of mental disorder was proved by the accused or where she was found to be unfit for trial. These include a "compulsion order", which authorises detention in a hospital, and the option of making no order whatsoever.

The case of *Thomson* v *HM Advocate* (1999) demonstrates some of the criteria which the courts use in deciding which disposal is appropriate, a decision which is not based solely on the accused's welfare. In this case, the decision to impose a "restriction order" was upheld on appeal.

VOLUNTARY INTOXICATION

Scots law does not accept voluntary intoxication as a defence to any charge. This follows from Hume's trenchant views on the subject:

> "... certain it is, that the law of Scotland views this wilful distemper with a quite different eye from the other, which is the visitation of Providence; and if it does not consider the man's intemperance as an aggravation, at least sees very good reasons why it should not be allowed as an excuse, to save him from the ordinary pains of his transgression" (i, 45).

The current law on voluntary intoxication, which is again to be found in *Brennan* v *HM Advocate* (1977), restates this basic principle. The law's view on voluntary intoxication is that it is an act of recklessness, in itself, to go out and deliberately become intoxicated. Accordingly, if the mental element of the particular crime libelled is any form of recklessness, voluntary intoxication cannot be a defence. In fact, this principle has been extended to all crimes, no matter what the mental element. As Lord Justice-General Hope stated in *Ross* v *HM Advocate* (1991), "any defence based upon the argument that self-induced intoxication has resulted in the absence of *mens rea*" (at 214) is excluded in Scots law. This is the prevailing view because, in such cases, "the accused must be assumed to have intended the natural consequences of his act" (at 214).

AUTOMATISM

The criminal law seeks to punish only voluntary actions – or actions which the accused would have been able to avoid committing.

The defence of automatism is concerned with involuntary actions – actions where, although the accused was the agent who carried them out, it is recognised that it would have been impossible for him or her to have avoided doing so.

The law is currently as set down in the case of *Ross* v *HM Advocate* (1991). Ross had gone berserk with a knife and had seriously injured various people, most of whom were complete strangers to him. It was established that he had been drinking lager from a can but that, *unknown to him*, five or six tablets of temazepam and some LSD had also been squeezed into the can.

The court recognised the inherent unfairness of convicting some-one in these circumstances. It therefore resurrected a defence which had previously been recognised by Scots law in the 1920s – that of "non-insane automatism". Following *Ross*, four conditions must be satisfied in order to establish the defence:

(1) the accused must have been suffering from a total alienation of reason rendering him incapable of controlling or appreciating what he was doing;

(2) such alienation must have been caused by an external factor;

(3) that factor must not have been self-induced;

(4) the factor must also not be one which the accused was bound to foresee.

As all of these conditions were satisfied, it was held that Ross had no *mens rea* and he was therefore acquitted.

Following *Sorley* v *HM Advocate* (1992), it is clear that direct evidence on all four of these points is required before an accused can be acquitted. In that case, no expert medical evidence was led as to the effect which LSD in a can of lager would have on the accused. Accordingly, the court took the view that it had no evidence either that there was a causative link between the ingestion of LSD and the accused's mental state or that that mental state amounted to the total alienation of reason. The defence of automatism therefore failed.

The strictness of the tests laid down in *Ross* was again affirmed in *Cardle* v *Mulrainey* (1992), where amphetamines were introduced into the accused's lager without his knowledge. This led him to commit a series of criminal acts in a short space of time. He knew that these acts were wrong but he claimed that the effect of the amphetamine was to rob him of the ability to stop himself. The High Court held that, because he retained that level of knowledge of the wrongness of his acts, he was not suffering from a total alienation of his reason.

The defence will not assist those who take drugs for a legitimate purpose if they take more than the stated dose. In *Ebsworth* v *HM Advocate* (1992), the accused had a broken leg and there was some difficulty in uniting the fracture. To deal with the pain, he had taken 50 paracetamol and 10 diamorphine tablets. He claimed that he did not have the necessary *mens rea* for the offence of assault to severe disfigurement.

The court held that taking such a large quantity of these drugs was reckless in itself and that therefore the defence of automatism was not open to him. However, it did also state that, *normally*, if drugs were taken for a legitimate purpose, this would not deprive an accused of the defence of automatism, provided there was no recklessness, even though the cause of the alienation of reason in those circumstances would have been self-induced.

Thus, if the drugs were legal and the accused followed the dosage instructions properly, they *would* be able to use the defence of automatism.

External factors

The judgment in *Ross* does not define "external factor" but it appears to mean something which the accused inhaled or consumed or ingested or perhaps something which happened to him, such as a blow to the head inducing concussion. In *Ross*, it was suggested that an anaesthetic administered for a proper medical or dental purpose could also be regarded as an external factor.

Internal factors

It is also possible that a factor *internal* to an accused might cause him or her to act criminally in circumstances which he or she cannot control but where the mental state falls short of insanity – for example, those in a hypoglycaemic state arising from diabetes, or people suffering from epilepsy. The basic rule is that, apart from non-insane automatism on the *Ross* model:

> "[a]ny mental or pathological condition short of insanity – any question of diminished responsibility owing to any cause, which does not involve insanity – is relevant only to the question of mitigating circumstances and sentence" (*HM Advocate* v *Cunningham* (1963), per Lord Justice-General Clyde at 84).

However, there is some disquiet over the position into which this puts diabetics in particular. It seems unreasonable to classify diabetes as a form of insanity (or mental disorder) yet, to have a complete defence to an act committed while experiencing a hypoglycaemic episode, the accused would have to meet the legal test for this.

The case of *MacLeod* v *Mathieson* (1993) dealt with diabetic hypo-glycaemia. It should be noted that this is only a sheriff court decision, but that it was taken subsequent to the High Court's decision in *Ross* v *HM Advocate* (1991).

The accused was charged with careless driving, which caused an accident in which another motorist died. At the time of the offence the accused, who was a diabetic, was suffering a hypoglycaemic attack. The sheriff applied the four tests set down in *Ross*. He accepted *expressly* that a hypoglycaemic attack could constitute an external factor. However, he decided that, because the accused had previously been diagnosed as diabetic, and therefore knew that he was prone to hypoglycaemic attacks, it could not be argued that *this* attack was unforeseeable. Accordingly, the accused failed the fourth of the *Ross* tests and was convicted.

Somnambulism

The early case of *HM Advocate* v *Simon Fraser* (1878) treats a crime committed while the accused was in a state of wakeful unconsciousness – ie sleepwalking with his eyes open – in a particular way. In that case, Fraser killed his 18-month-old child while sleepwalking. Fraser was found guilty but released on signing an undertaking that he would always sleep on his own.

In the more recent case of *Finegan* v *Heywood* (2000), the accused had been out celebrating the birth of his baby and had consumed at least six pints of beer. He had gone home and fallen asleep, then, in a state of "parasomnia", taken his friend's car keys and driven his (the friend's) car. He was convicted of a motoring offence. On appeal, the High Court held that he could not use the defence of non-insane automatism because he knew that drinking alcohol induced sleepwalking, therefore he himself had brought about the circumstances which caused him to commit the crime. However, the court did not see any reason why parasomnia which was not self-induced should not ground a plea of non-insane automatism in the future.

COERCION

Some commentators examine the defences of coercion and necessity together as a species of duress. Here they will be examined separately. Effectively, coercion arises where one person has forced another to commit a crime. There is still debate as to whether coercion can ever be used as a defence to murder. The point has not, as yet, been conclusively tested in Scotland.

The law on coercion is still based on a passage in Hume at i, 53:

"But generally, and with relation to the ordinary condition of a well-regulated society, where every man is under the shield of the law, and has the means of resorting to that protection, this is at least somewhat a difficult plea, and can hardly be serviceable in the case of a trial for any atrocious crime, unless it have the support of these qualifications: an immediate danger of death or great bodily harm; an inability to resist the violence; a backward and inferior part in the perpetration; and a disclosure of the fact, as well as restitution of the spoil, on the first safe and convenient occasion. For if the pannel take a very active part in the enterprise, or conceal the fact and detain his share of the profit, when restored to a state of freedom, either of these replies will serve in a great measure to elide his defence."

Effectively, then, in this passage, Hume sets down four tests to establish coercion in Scots law:

(1) an *immediate* danger of death or great bodily harm;
(2) an inability to resist the violence;

(3) a backward and inferior part in the perpetration; and

(4) a disclosure of the fact as well as restitution of the spoil.

In *Thomson* v *HM Advocate* (1983), in deciding Thomson's appeal against conviction, the High Court indicated that only the first two tests are *essential* to the establishment of the defence. The other two tests "come into play as measures of the accused's credibility and reliability on the issue of the defence" (per Lord Justice-Clerk Wheatley at 78).

Immediate danger

Hume specifies that the threat must be *immediate*. Difficulty arises where threats of *future* harm, either to the accused or, perhaps, to members of his family are made. In the case of *Thomson* v *HM Advocate* (1983), a man took part in the robbery of a Post Office sorting office, according to him, unwillingly.

Lord Wheatley stated (at 77): "'[i]mmediate danger' may have to be construed in the circumstances in which it is threatened, but clearly if there is the opportunity to run away or to seek the protection of the forces of law and order before the crime is committed, then the accused cannot claim to have been coerced."

Inability to resist the violence

If made out to the jury's satisfaction, coercion is a complete defence. The accused generally has to make a decision to act – ie to weigh up the danger of the threat being carried out against his or her desire not to commit the crime. Scots law takes the view that the will of the coerced person must be completely overborne before a defence of coercion can succeed.

The charge of the trial judge to the jury in *HM Advocate* v *Raiker and Others* (1989) indicates that Scots criminal law approaches the situation where the will of the accused has been completely overborne by the threat as an indication that the accused lacks the *mens rea* for the offence.

Cochrane v *HM Advocate* (2001) deals specifically with the issue of overcoming the accused's will. In particular, it considers whether the test of coercion is an objective or a subjective one. In other words, is the issue whether the will of the accused personally, with all of his or her existing characteristics, has been overcome (ie a subjective test)? Alternatively, is the question whether the will of an "ordinary person" in the position of the accused would have been overcome (ie an objective test)?

The facts of *Cochrane* were that the accused had entered the home of the complainer while she was sleeping in a chair. When she woke up, he threatened her with a candlestick if she did not hand over her purse to him. She refused and he hit her three or four times on the head with the candlestick so that she eventually gave him the purse. He stole her wages.

Cochrane claimed that he had been coerced into carrying out the attack by a co-accused who had threatened to blow up Cochrane's house and to "hammer" him. It was established in evidence that Cochrane's IQ placed him in the bottom 4 per cent of the population and that he was "highly compliant". This meant that he was very easily led by other people.

In deciding Cochrane's appeal against conviction, the High Court considered whether the accused's particular suggestibility was relevant. It held that it was not. Thus, for coercion, in deciding whether the accused was justified in giving in to the threat, the question is "whether an ordinary sober person of reasonable firmness, sharing the characteristics of the accused, would have responded as the accused did" (per Lord Justice-General Rodger at para 29). This applies even if the accused, as an individual, is manifestly not such a person.

NECESSITY

Until recently, the use and scope of the defence of necessity was unclear. Famous old English and American cases had rejected it. In the cannibalism case of *R v Dudley and Stephens* (1884), where shipwrecked sailors killed and ate the cabin boy in order to save their own lives, it was unsuccessful. Again, in another shipwreck case – *US v Holmes* (1842) – the defence was rejected where a sailor threw about 14 passengers out of a lifeboat in an attempt to lighten its load so that everyone else would survive.

In modern Scots law, most of the attempts to make use of the defence have related to road traffic cases. The case of *Moss* v *Howdle* (1997) sets down clearly the circumstances in which it can be used. In that case, the accused, Moss, was spotted by the police driving down the M74 at a speed in excess of 100 mph where the speed limit was 70 mph. Moss left the motorway at the Gretna services area and was there charged with speeding. Moss's explanation was that his passenger (a man named Pearson) had suddenly started to shout out in extreme pain. Moss had taken the view that Pearson was seriously ill and that the best way to ensure that he received assistance was to get to the nearest service station as quickly as possible. Pearson was, in fact, only suffering from a bad attack of cramp, although it was accepted that Moss was entitled to form the view that Pearson's condition was much more serious because of Pearson's reaction to it.

Moss had considered using his mobile phone to call for help but had remembered that the battery was flat. The sheriff's findings in fact affirmed this version of events but also noted that Moss had had the option of pulling in to the side of the road, assessing the situation and summoning help from there, if necessary. Because there was a viable option available to Moss, which did not involve breaking the law, the sheriff rejected the defence of necessity and convicted him.

On appeal, the High Court upheld the sheriff's decision but its judgment is particularly important because it sets down the scope of the defence of necessity in Scots law. It is also interesting because it conflates, to some extent, the rules of coercion with those of necessity and refers to this in some places as the defence of "duress". Five important points emerge from the High Court's judgment in *Moss* v *Howdle* (1997):

(1) the defence of necessity is available in respect of all offences. It does not matter whether these are strict liability or require *mens rea*;

(2) the minimum requirement of the defence is that the accused acted in the face of immediate danger of death or great bodily harm;

(3) the danger from which the accused is escaping can consist in either threats of physical violence, or natural phenomena such as flood or serious illness;

(4) it does not matter if the immediate danger is to the accused him- or herself or to their companion. It is equally appropriate to act to save a companion;

(5) if there is a viable alternative course of action which the accused could have taken and which would not have involved committing the offence, then they must do this. The defence of necessity will not be available where they have failed to do so. It was for this reason that Moss's attempt to use the defence failed. He should have stopped by the side of the road and assessed the situation.

These rules were applied in the subsequent case of *Ruxton* v *Lang* (1998), where, after a night out during which she had consumed a large quantity of alcohol, the accused drove because her ex-boyfriend had threatened her with a knife in her own home. It was held that, when she started driving, she would have been able to use the defence of necessity but that, by the time she was stopped by the police, the immediate danger had passed and that she should have stopped driving as soon as she knew her ex-boyfriend was not following.

The strictness of these tests is also apparent from the recent case of
D v *Donnelly* (2009). Here, the accused was indecently assaulted in the
car park of a social club. She had drunk alcohol earlier in the evening,
intending not to drive thereafter. After the assault, she was distressed and
she drove to get away from her assailants. It was held that, at the time
when she drove, the last of the assailants had left the locus therefore she
was not in *immediate* danger of great bodily harm. Also, there was a viable
alternative course of action open to her, in that she could have called for
help on her mobile. The defence of necessity was not available in these
circumstances.

Dawson v *McKay* (1999) also applied the *Moss* tests. In that case the
accused was employed as a firefighter. On the night in question, he was *not*
on call but he had been out in the pub with a colleague who was. A call
came through for Dawson's companion to attend a serious road accident
and Dawson decided to go too. He drove a fire engine to the scene. He
was assisting with the use of cutting equipment when an ambulance driver
shouted that the fire engine which Dawson had driven had to be moved.
It was blocking the exit of an ambulance carrying a critically injured
patient.

Without giving the matter any thought, Dawson reversed the fire
engine – into a police car. The police officer driving the car breathalysed
him and he was found to have over twice the legal limit of alcohol in his
blood. He was charged with driving with excess alcohol in his breath
and pled necessity. His argument was that, if he had not moved the fire
engine immediately, the person in the ambulance might have died. The
court took the view that the defence of necessity was not available to
Dawson. It stated that the accused must have weighed up the risk which
he was seeking to avoid (delaying the ambulance's departure) against the
fact that he was going to break the law. In this instance, it was clear from
Dawson's evidence that he would have driven anyway and that he had
not considered any other options such as getting another driver to move
the fire engine. His mind was not dominated by the extreme urgency of
the situation. Accordingly, he was convicted.

As a result of *Moss* v *Howdle* (1997), the defences of coercion and
necessity are now very difficult to separate out from each other.

NON-AGE

A child who is below the age of criminal responsibility cannot be
prosecuted for any offence, nor can he or she be referred to a children's
panel on the ground that they have committed an offence (*Merrin* v *S*

(1987)). This is set down in s 41 of the Criminal Procedure (Scotland) Act 1995: "[i]t shall be conclusively presumed that no child under the age of eight years can be guilty of any offence".

Accordingly, anyone aged 7 or under who is charged with a criminal offence has a complete defence. The Criminal Justice and Licensing (Scotland) Bill, s 38 will amend the law in this area so that it will be impossible to prosecute a child aged between 8 and 11 (inclusive) in the (adult) courts but she could still be referred to a children's hearing on the ground that she has committed an offence.

Essential Facts

- The special defences currently recognised by Scots law are alibi, incrimination, insanity, self-defence, necessity, coercion and consent to certain sex offences. The accused must give prior notice of his intention to plead any of these. (On enactment of the Criminal Justice and Licensing (Scotland) Bill ("CJL(S)B"), the special defence of insanity will be abolished and replaced by mental disorder.)

- The burden of proof remains on the Crown throughout, except in the case of insanity (or mental disorder) which must be proved by the accused on the balance of probabilities.

- Insanity in bar of trial is pled where the accused is not fit to instruct a defence or to follow the proceedings in court. Such inability may have a mental or, in certain circumstances, a physical, cause. Evidence from two medical practitioners is required.

- On enactment of the CJL(S)B, insanity in bar of trial will be abolished and replaced by the plea of unfitness for trial, the test for which will be that the accused is incapable, by reason of a mental or physical condition, of participating effectively in a trial. In determining whether the accused is capable of effective participation, the CJL(S)B sets down five specific, and one general, factor to which the court is to have regard, related to the accused's understanding of aspects of the matter and his ability to instruct and communicate with his legal representative. Unfitness for trial must be proved on the balance of probabilities.

- Both at common law and under the CJL(S)B's provisions, if the relevant plea is successful, an examination of the facts is held, in lieu of a trial, to determine whether or not the accused committed the crime and, if so, whether there are any grounds for acquitting him.

- If insanity is made out as a special defence, it leads to acquittal. It requires proof of total alienation of reason, in relation to the actual offence with which the accused is charged, arising from mental illness, mental disease or defect or unsoundness of mind. Only the accused will be able to plead the (new) special defence of mental disorder. If established, it will lead to acquittal. The accused will be required to prove, on the balance of probabilities, that she is unable, by reason of mental disorder, to appreciate the nature or wrongfulness of the conduct.

- Insanity is a purely legal concept. Medical evidence is only one element of the evidence which may be considered in determining whether the accused satisfies the test for insanity.

- If the accused is found to be insane, there are six possible disposals available to the court, including compulsory detention in a hospital. This will remain unchanged on enactment of the provisions on mental disorder and unfitness for trial in the CJL(S)B.

- Voluntary intoxication is no defence to any crime in Scots criminal law.

- An accused can make use of the defence of automatism where he or she has suffered a total alienation of reason caused by an external factor which was neither self-induced nor foreseeable. The most common example is where a drink has been "spiked" with drugs.

- There must be direct evidence on all four of the foregoing points and the accused must establish that the alienation of reason was total. Retention of any rational control over the acts will be fatal to the defence. The defence may be available where the accused has an unforeseen reaction to legal drugs, unless these have not been taken according to instructions.

- The defence of coercion is available where the accused has been subjected to a threat of immediate danger of death or great bodily harm such that he or she is unable to resist the violence. Their will must have been completely overcome. It is helpful in establishing the accused's credibility and the reliability of the defence if they have taken a more minor role in the commission of the crime and have informed the police and returned any proceeds at the first possible opportunity.

- For the purposes of establishing the defence, the accused must be regarded as an ordinary sober person of reasonable firmness but, otherwise, as having all of his or her own characteristics. Neither excessive courage nor excessive timidity will be taken into account just because the accused in fact possesses these characteristics.

- The defence of necessity is available in relation to all crimes. The accused must have been subjected to a threat of immediate danger of death or great bodily harm, whether to herself or to a companion and whether at the hands of another person or from natural or medical causes. If there is a viable alternative course of action which is also legal then the defence will fail.

- The defence cannot be used once the danger has ceased. The defence can be used only where the accused has weighed up the undesirability of committing the crime against the danger which will be averted by acting illegally.

- It is a complete defence to any charge that the accused is aged 7 or under.

Essential Cases

Lambie v HM Advocate (1973): insanity is the only special defence where the burden of proof shifts on to the accused, on the balance of probabilities.

HM Advocate v Wilson (1942): the test for insanity in bar of trial at common law is whether the accused is fit to instruct a defence and to follow the proceedings in court.

Brennan v HM Advocate (1977): the test for insanity as a special defence at common law is that the accused is suffering from a total alienation of reason in relation to the act charged arising from mental illness, mental disease or defect or unsoundness of mind. Voluntary intoxication is no defence to any crime in Scots criminal law.

Ross v HM Advocate (1991): automatism is established where the accused suffers a total alienation of reason caused by an external factor which was neither self-induced nor foreseeable.

Sorley v HM Advocate (1992): direct evidence must be led in order to satisfy all four of the tests set down in *Ross* before automatism is established.

Cardle v Mulrainey (1992): if the accused retains any rational control or understanding of his or her actions, the alienation of reason is not total and the defence of automatism will be unsuccessful.

Ebsworth v HM Advocate (1992): an adverse reaction to legal drugs used according to instructions may ground a defence of automatism.

Thomson v HM Advocate (1983): coercion requires an immediate threat of danger of death or great bodily harm and an inability to resist that violence.

HM Advocate v Raiker and Others (1989): where the accused's will has been completely overborne by an immediate threat, he or she will lack *mens rea*.

Cochrane v HM Advocate (2001): in determining whether the accused has been coerced, he or she must be regarded by the jury as an ordinary sober person of reasonable firmness, sharing the accused's other characteristics.

Moss v Howdle (1997): to establish the defence of necessity, the accused, or a companion, must have been in immediate danger of death or great bodily harm, whether arising from another person, illness or a natural phenomenon. If the accused has failed to take a viable, alternative, legal course of action, the defence cannot be made out.

Ruxton v Lang (1998): necessity cannot be used once the danger has ceased.

Dawson v McKay (1999): if the accused would have acted anyway, without weighing up the illegality against the danger to be averted, the defence is unavailable.

8 ASSAULT

The classic definition of assault is provided by Macdonald: "assault is constituted by any deliberate attack upon the person of another, whether or not actual injury be inflicted" (115).

ACTUS REUS

The *actus reus* of assault is an attack on someone else. Words alone cannot constitute an attack. The common law proscribes separately, and as an offence in its own right, making certain kinds of serious threat. This was the charge in *MacKellar* v *Dickson* (1898) where the accused issued two written death threats.

What can constitute an attack? In *Lachlan Brown* (1842) setting fire to a piece of paper in the victim's hand while the victim slept amounted to an attack. Gordon (at para 29.01) indicates that it is an attack to slap someone on the back or possibly even to tap him on the shoulder or to spit on him.

There is no need for the attack to cause injury.

Indirect attacks

Assault can be committed indirectly, so that, instead of the accused actually attacking the victim, he or she causes something or someone else to do so. In *Quinn* v *Lees* (1994) setting a dog on a group of boys constituted an assault. Similarly, in *David Keay* (1837), the accused was riding in a carriage and whipped a pony as he overtook it. The pony bolted and threw its rider who was seriously injured.

Menaces

We have seen that words are not enough to constitute the *actus reus* of assault. Threatening gestures or menaces, which may or may not be accompanied by words, do, however, come within the ambit of an attack for the purposes of assault. In *Atkinson* v *HM Advocate* (1987), Atkinson and a co-accused named Kennedy had broken into the shop at a petrol station in Saltcoats. They had jumped over the counter, wearing masks, and "assaulted" the cashier, taking £798.73. The jury deleted part of the charge against Atkinson (which related to holding a knife against the cashier's neck) on the grounds that it was his co-accused who had done this and that that had gone beyond Atkinson's expectation of the level of violence to be used. On appeal, the High Court held that Atkinson was still guilty of assault because "[a]n assault may be constituted by threatening gestures sufficient to produce alarm" (per Lord Justice-Clerk Ross at 535).

MENS REA

The *mens rea* of assault is "evil intent". "Evil intent" is usually taken to mean that the accused's intention was to cause harm to the victim. This point was clarified in the case of *Smart* v *HM Advocate* (1975):

> "[a]n assault is an attack on the person of another. Evil intention is of the essence of assault . . . So too if persons engage in sporting activities governed by rules, then, although some form of violence may be involved within the rules, there is no assault because the intention is to engage in the sporting activity and not evilly to do harm to the opponent" (per Lord Justice-Clerk Wheatley at 33).

In *Smart*, the accused and the victim had agreed to have a "square go". The accused sought to rely on this as a defence but the court held that it was clear that he had fought with the victim with intent to injure and do bodily harm, therefore the *mens rea* of assault was satisfied. In fact, this intent is, in some respects, the essence of the "square go".

In *Lord Advocate's Reference (No 2 of 1992)* (1993), the High Court took a slightly different approach. The accused entered a babywear shop in Glasgow and presented an imitation firearm at the proprietor. He demanded money from her and demanded that she lie on the ground. When another assistant, who had been bending down, trying to put a jacket on a little boy, stood up, the accused ran off. He claimed that, as he was leaving, he said "I'm only kidding" and laughed. He admitted that he had carried out these acts and had caused the shopkeepers to be alarmed.

At his trial, his defence was that he had carried out these actions as a joke and the sheriff directed the jury that, if they believed it was a joke, they should acquit because, almost by definition, a joke could not constitute "evil intention". The jury duly acquitted on that basis.

The Lord Advocate referred the point of law – the question of the *mens rea* for assault – to the High Court. It held that it was clear that the accused's assertion that this was a joke meant no more than that this was his motive in carrying it out. Since the accused acted deliberately (rather than negligently or carelessly) in pointing the gun and speaking as he did, he had the necessary intention to satisfy the *mens rea* of assault.

It therefore appears that acting deliberately, in the knowledge that the action will cause alarm and distress, is sufficient to constitute the *mens rea* of assault, without, necessarily, the requirement of intention to cause immediate bodily injury, or the fear of it.

Transferred intent

The issue of transferred intent arises where the accused intended to assault one person but accidentally hit another instead. It was recognised expressly by Hume (i, 22) who took the view that the intention to injure one person was sufficient evidence of the existence of dole.

Two modern Scottish cases have dealt with this issue. In *Connor* v *Jessop* (1988), the accused was involved in a fight at a disco in Glasgow. He threw a glass at one of his opponents but it missed and struck the complainer on the foot, causing an injury which required 12 stitches. In *Roberts* v *Hamilton* (1989), most of the protagonists had attended a funeral tea in Dunfermline at which much alcohol had been consumed. The accused swung a clothes pole at her partner, who was involved in a fight with her son, but, instead, made contact with the hand of a third party, fracturing his little finger.

In both cases, the High Court held that the crime of assault was established because the accused had evil intent and had attacked someone – albeit not the intended victim.

AGGRAVATED ASSAULT

There are a number of aggravations – circumstances which render it a more serious offence – of the crime of assault. Examples include the use of a weapon or the outcome of the attack. The charge may, for example, allege that the assault was "to the severe injury" or "to the permanent disfigurement" or "to the danger of life".

In terms of para 9(3) of Sch 3 to the Criminal Procedure (Scotland) Act 1995, if the Crown is unable to prove the aggravating circumstances beyond reasonable doubt, it may still be able to obtain a conviction for the basic offence. Proof of the aggravation is of most relevance in relation to sentencing.

LEGITIMATE VIOLENCE

There are certain circumstances in which an action which would otherwise constitute an assault is not viewed as criminal:

(1) Violence permitted by virtue of office

The law sometimes permits certain officials, such as police officers, to use violence in particular circumstances. In *Brown v Hilson* (1924), Lord Sands stated: "It happens from time to time that charges of assault are made against officials and others who are entitled, in virtue of their office, to exercise in certain circumstances physical force. I may cite as examples police officers, prison warders, asylum attendants, railway servants, and ships' officers" (at 6). Currently, it appears that, at common law, bouncers are allowed to use violence in this way, though this is not absolutely settled. In *HM Advocate* v *Harris* (1993), the accused was a bouncer who ejected a woman from a nightclub in the course of his employment. A surprising aspect of the case is that all of the judges, except one, seemed simply to accept that bouncers might be justified in using violence by virtue of their office. Lord McCluskey, who dissented, stated, however, that "[t]here is not one law for bouncers and another law for the rest" (at 161).

In order for the violence not to constitute an assault, two conditions must be satisfied:

(1) the individual must have been acting by virtue of his or her office; and

(2) the violence used must have been no more than is reasonable or necessary in all the circumstances.

In *McLean* v *Jessop* (1989), the accused was a police officer who had hit the victim over the head with his baton. The accused had responded to a call about an alleged housebreaking and had taken the view that the victim was running away. In fact, he was the householder who had called the police. The High Court held that the police officer had good reason to think that the complainer was implicated in the housebreaking and that he was clearly trying to secure his arrest when he used his baton.

(2) Citizen's arrest

The basic requirements of a citizen's arrest are:

(1) that the arrester should have information gained by, or equivalent to, personal observation that the arrestee is indeed responsible for the crime;

(2) that no more than reasonable force should be used.

In *Codona* v *Cardle* (1989), the window of an amusement arcade, of which the accused was a co-owner, had been broken. The accused was not present when this occurred. He arrived shortly afterwards and drove one of his employees, who had been in the arcade at the time, around the town to try to identify the person who had broken the window. The employee eventually pointed out a man named David Freke and the accused told Freke that he was effecting a citizen's arrest for breaking the window. Freke refused to go with the accused who then twisted Freke's arm up his back forcefully and painfully. The accused was charged with assault.

He was convicted and this was upheld on appeal. The High Court stated that the accused did not have the necessary first-hand, personal knowledge that the victim had committed the crime of breaking the window. Even if he did satisfy the first criterion, the force used had been excessive, therefore his conviction of assault should stand.

In *Wightman* v *Lees* (2000), the arrest was effected by a citizen who had not actually seen the crime (theft of a drill) but had encountered the thief on his way out of the premises from which the drill had been stolen. The thief had given an obviously untrue reason for his presence there and had then run away. The court held that the whole circumstances were so incriminating that the citizen had what amounted to a moral certainty that the accused had committed a crime. Anything less than this would not, however, justify a citizen in taking action.

(3) Reasonable chastisement

Currently, parents are permitted to perform acts which would, in other circumstances constitute assaults, if these are carried out as "reasonable chastisement" for a misdemeanour committed by the child. This right is limited by s 51 of the Criminal Justice (Scotland) Act 2003. Prior to the Act, the primary issue had always been the parent's *mens rea* – whether or not he had the evil intent necessary for assault. In the more recent cases, this had been determined on an objective basis – by inference from the surrounding circumstances – rather than subjectively, in terms of what the parent claimed his own intention had been. In G v *Templeton* (1998), the court said that "the relevant issue is not the state of mind of the parent, but whether the punishment, viewed objectively, exceeded what was reasonable" (per Sheriff Principal Risk at 184). In this case the accused had slapped his 15-year-old daughter on the face following an argument involving a number of family members. This was held not to be reasonable chastisement.

Section 51 follows this approach and concentrates on the effect which the chastisement has on the child. Blows to the head, shaking and the use of an implement to inflict the punishment can never be reasonable chastisement.

OTHER DEFENCES TO A CHARGE OF ASSAULT

Self-defence (of people)

This is a valid and complete defence to a charge of assault. Its principles are discussed fully in Chapter 10: Homicide.

Self-defence (of property)

It is unclear whether or not this constitutes a defence to a charge of assault. If it is a valid defence, the accused must not use excessive or unreasonable force but the measure of this, given that the accused will have attacked a person in defence of property, is unclear.

Victim's consent

The leading case on the victim's consent is *Smart* v *HM Advocate* (1975) – the "square go" case. Smart had challenged the victim, Wilkie, to a "square go" and Wilkie had accepted the challenge. The court was unequivocal in its view that, if the attack was carried out with evil intent, the victim's consent to the injuries inflicted did not negate the assault.

On the other hand, consent to a medical examination can be taken to negate the *mens rea* where a medical practitioner carries out an examination which would otherwise constitute an assault. The consent only relates to the specific examination to be carried out. In *Hussain* v *Houston* (1995), there were three complainers, one of whom had injured her thumb. The accused did not examine the thumb but placed his hand under her clothing and fondled her breasts and private parts. It was held that this constituted an assault.

In sport, if the violence falls outwith the rules, then it is possible to bring an assault charge. In *Ferguson* v *Normand* (1995), the footballer Duncan Ferguson headbutted an opponent in the course of a match. He was convicted of assault.

Provocation

This is not a defence to assault but may be relevant to sentence.

Essential Facts

- Assault is an attack (which does not have to cause injury) upon someone else, carried out with the *mens rea* of evil intent. It has been held that carrying out an attack deliberately, in the knowledge that it will cause distress, is enough to constitute an assault, without, necessarily, a clear intention to harm the victim or make him think that he will be harmed. Words alone cannot constitute an attack.

- The attack may be carried out indirectly, as, for example, by causing an animal to bite.

- Threatening gestures or menaces, whether or not accompanied by words, are sufficient to constitute the *actus reus*.

- The doctrine of transferred intent applies. Where A intends to attack B but misses and injures C, A is still guilty of assaulting C.

- In certain circumstances the law allows violence to be used so that no assault is committed. The most common categories are the use of violence by virtue of an office held, such as police officer; citizen's arrest; and reasonable chastisement of children. All are strictly circumscribed.

- Self-defence is a complete defence to a charge of assault. Evidence of provocation may be led but is relevant only to sentence.

Essential Cases

Atkinson v HM Advocate (1987): threatening gestures or menaces are sufficient to constitute the *actus reus* of assault.

Smart v HM Advocate (1975): the *mens rea* of assault is evil intent to harm the victim. The fact that the victim consents to the risk of harm (as in this case where the accused and the victim were involved in a "square go" outside a pub) is irrelevant.

Lord Advocate's Reference (No 2 of 1992) (1993): the accused's motive in carrying out an attack (here he claimed it was a joke) is irrelevant. If an attack is carried out deliberately and in the knowledge that it will cause alarm and distress, the *mens rea* requirement for assault is satisfied.

Connor v Jessop (1988) and **Roberts v Hamilton (1989)**: the doctrine of transferred intent applies in assault.

Codona v Cardle (1989): to effect a citizen's arrest, the accused must actually have witnessed the crime and must use no more than reasonable force.

Wightman v Lees (2000): if the accused has a "moral certainty" that the accused is the perpetrator of a crime, this is sufficient to allow him to effect a citizen's arrest, even if he did not actually witness the offence.

G v Templeton (1998): the courts will take an objective approach to the question of whether a parent actually had the *mens rea* for assault in cases of reasonable chastisement of children.

9 NON-FATAL CRIMES OF RECKLESSNESS AGAINST THE PERSON

At base, recklessness involves an unacceptable level of risk-taking – doing something which is so risky that it might cause serious harm to others without taking the precautions which would mitigate that risk. In essence, it requires a very serious disregard for the consequences of one's actions.

SUBJECTIVE OR OBJECTIVE RECKLESSNESS

With regard to recklessness as a *mens rea* generally, there has been much debate as to whether the law requires subjective recklessness or objective recklessness.

Subjective recklessness arises where the accused knew that there was a risk but disregarded it.

Objective recklessness arises where the reasonable person would have realised that there was a risk. It is likely to include circumstances where the accused gave no thought to the risk at all but clearly there was one. To that extent, then, objective recklessness is judged by an outsider's perception of the risk rather than by what the accused actually thought.

It has been said that the Scottish courts usually hold to an objective standard of recklessness however the matter is not entirely clearcut and there are *dicta* pointing both ways.

APPLYING RECKLESSNESS

In *Quinn* v *Cunningham* (1956) the accused was charged with riding a bicycle in a reckless manner so that it knocked down a pedestrian. Both the accused and the pedestrian sustained slight injuries. The complaint was held to be irrelevant for technical reasons but, in the course of the case, certain comments were made on the issue of recklessness. The court defined recklessness as "an utter disregard of what the consequences of the act in question may be so far as the public are concerned" (per Lord Justice-General Clyde at 24). It does not, however, indicate from whose perspective the existence of that "utter disregard" is to be judged. Must the accused himself have – subjectively – recognised the risk and chosen utterly to disregard it or is it an objective standard so that, if a reasonable person would conclude that the consequences as far as the public were concerned had been utterly disregarded, the accused has been criminally reckless? The court went on to state that the standard of recklessness set down in *Paton* v *HM Advocate* (1936) (discussed below) should apply in all recklessness cases – not just those in which death resulted from the reckless behaviour (at 24–25). Further on in the case, the standard of recklessness is restated as "recklessness so high as to involve an indifference to the consequences for the public generally" (per Lord Justice-General Clyde at 25).

The court also clarified that there is a clear difference between recklessness (the standard required for culpability in the criminal law) and negligence or carelessness (the standard which applies in the civil law) (per Lord Sorn at 26).

"PATON" RECKLESSNESS

The definition of recklessness which is now generally applied in common law crimes comes from the case of *Paton* v *HM Advocate* (1936). The charge in this case was culpable homicide arising from reckless driving. The court defined recklessness as: "gross, or wicked, or criminal negligence; something amounting, or at any rate analogous, to a criminal indifference to consequences" (per Lord Justice-Clerk Aitchison at 22).

Some criticism of the circularity inherent in the *Paton* definition is evident from the judgment in *Transco plc* v *HM Advocate* (2004), particularly in relation to the use, on two occasions, of the word "criminal" in a definition which is supposed to be explaining what the criminal standard is. Nonetheless, Lord Osborne (at 33) accepts that the phrase "gross or wicked indifference to consequences" (arrived at by removing the references to "criminal" from the original statement) is helpful. Lord Hamilton (at 48) considers that the *Paton* definition points to a degree of want of care which is grave.

Overall, the words "gross" and "wicked" (and, indeed, "criminal") are strong. This indicates that a high degree of indifference is necessary.

There are three main crimes involving personal injury which can be committed recklessly:

(1) RECKLESSLY CAUSING INJURY

Until the case of *HM Advocate* v *Harris* (1993), it had been thought that it was necessary for the "lieges" (in other words the general public as a group – or those who happen to be present at the time of the offence) to be put at risk by the accused's actions before causing injury by a reckless act would constitute a criminal offence. In *Harris*, the charge did not allege that the action taken was "to the danger of the lieges" and, accordingly, the defence sought to have the whole case dismissed.

The accused was the bouncer at Tin Pan Alley, a nightclub in Glasgow. He was charged with culpably, wilfully and recklessly seizing hold of his victim, pushing her on the body and causing her to fall down a flight of steps and onto the roadway, as a result of which she was struck by a motor vehicle to her severe injury and permanent disfigurement. The court held that causing a real injury by reckless conduct did constitute a crime.

(2) CULPABLY AND RECKLESSLY ENDANGERING THE LIEGES

The older crime, which is also still relevant in Scots criminal law, is culpably and recklessly endangering the lieges. This can be charged where no one has actually been injured as a result of the accused's actions, but it is still equally competent to charge it where there has been injury. Two cases illustrate the current approach of the High Court to this crime.

In *Robson* v *Spiers* (1999), the charge was culpably and recklessly chasing nine bullocks, causing them to escape onto a railway line, proceed along the railway line and then along a main road, thereby endangering persons using the railway line and the road. The accused was convicted (although he was only admonished) and he appealed against conviction. On appeal, it was held that it was sufficiently foreseeable, from the actions of the accused (and the others with him), that the bullocks would escape and endanger the public and the standard of "utter recklessness" (per Lord Kirkwood at 1144) required had been reached. The appeal was dismissed. Lord Kirkwood said, "If there was a material prospect of escape by the bullocks ... then the foreseeability of danger to the lieges was obvious" (at 1144). Again, as with the definition of recklessness found in *Quinn* v *Cunningham* (1956) it is not specifically stated to whom this danger should have been foreseeable – to the accused subjectively or to a reasonable onlooker.

Cameron v *Maguire* (1999) dealt with the reckless discharge of a firearm, in a relatively remote part of Mull, but near to an occupied house and a hotel. The court (per Lord Marnoch at 65–66) expressly approved the definition of "recklessness" as involving "an utter disregard of what the consequences of the act in question may be so far as the public are concerned" from *Quinn* v *Cunningham* (1956).

The accused was "zeroing" a new rifle – calibrating it so that, when he fired it, he would know where the bullet would land. An important point was that, because this was the first time he had used the gun, he did not yet have this knowledge. In his evidence, the accused indicated that he had thought it was safe to shoot but that, on looking at the situation again, he would not have done it a second time. Although this gives some indication that he had considered that there might be risk and the court took this into account, it does not seem to have placed much emphasis on it, stating that "it may not be wholly without significance" (per Lord Marnoch at 66). Accordingly, it appears that an objective standard operated here or, at the very least, that the test applied was not wholly subjective.

It is difficult, then, on the basis of the statements made by judges, to determine conclusively whether an objective or a subjective standard of recklessness predominates in Scots law. *Transco plc* v *HM Advocate* (2004) is clear that a "state of mind" (per Lord Osborne at 34, 35, 36; Lord Hamilton at 48, 49) is required. Lord Hamilton explained this more fully as follows: "a state of mind on the part of the accused which is 'wicked' or amounts, or is equivalent, to a complete indifference to the consequences of his conduct" (at 48–49). This, then, is an indication that the standard is subjective because, to constitute a state of mind, the accused must, by definition, have thought about the matter – of risk and/or consequences.

(3) CAUSING REAL INJURY

Causing real injury was resurrected in Scots law in the 1980s to deal with a specific social issue of the time – the sale of glue-sniffing kits. It is based on a passage from Hume (i, 327–328) where he argues that, if real injury is caused – even if it cannot come under any of the usual headings of "assault, invasion, beating and bruising, blooding and wounding, stabbing, mutilation [or] demembration" – then the act should still infer punishment.

The relevant case is *Khaliq* v *HM Advocate* (1984). The charge was that the accused had, from premises in the Saltmarket in Glasgow, "culpably, wilfully and recklessly" supplied children with quantities of solvents – usually Evostik – and the means to "sniff" them – tins, tubes and/or plastic bags. These items constituted glue-sniffing kits and the accused had carried out the supply knowing that the children intended to inhale the vapours and that this could be injurious to their health.

It was held that the act of supplying the kits was sufficient to constitute the crime libelled and the fact that the purchasers had themselves to act to cause the relevant injury did *not* constitute a *novus actus interveniens* in the chain of causation between the supply and the injury.

In *Ulhaq* v *HM Advocate* (1991), it was held that the fact that the victims in *Khaliq* were children was irrelevant. Supply to adults could equally constitute the charge.

This is a crime of recklessness. To satisfy the *mens rea* requirement, the accused must therefore have shown the requisite level of indifference to the consequences of his or her actions. It is also necessary, however, that the accused should *know* that the purchaser of the harmful item is likely to use it to harm him- or herself.

Essential Facts

- Recklessness involves acting in the face of an unacceptable level of risk, with utter disregard of the possible consequences.

- Subjective recklessness arises where the accused is aware of the risk but disregards it.

- Objective recklessness arises where a reasonable person would have realised that there was a risk and guarded against it.

- *Transco plc* v *HM Advocate* (2004) suggests that Scots law applies a subjective standard of recklessness, in its requirement for a "state of mind". Hitherto, there had been a view that it generally utilised an objective standard. The *dicta* in individual cases are ambiguous.

- The definition of recklessness generally applied is "gross, or wicked, or criminal negligence; something amounting, or at any rate analogous, to a criminal indifference to consequences". This may be more clearly expressed as "gross or wicked indifference to consequences" or as a degree of want of care which is grave.

- The crime of recklessly causing injury arises where the accused's reckless act injures another person.

- The crime of culpably and recklessly endangering the lieges arises where the accused's reckless act places those present at the time of the offence in danger.

- The crime of causing real injury arises where the accused's act is injurious to others, but not in a way which can be brought under the crime of assault, or recklessly causing injury. It has been used in relation to the sale of glue-sniffing kits, and to the distribution of drugs. As well as recklessness, the Crown must prove the accused's knowledge that the substance would be used in a way likely to cause harm to the victim.

Essential Cases

Quinn v Cunningham (1956): defines recklessness as "an utter disregard of what the consequences of the act in question may be so far as the public are concerned" (at 24) and "a recklessness so high as to involve an indifference to the consequences for the public generally" (at 25), definitions which are still sometimes used in modern cases.

Paton v HM Advocate (1936): provides the accepted definition of recklessness for common law crimes other than murder: "gross, or wicked, or criminal negligence; something amounting, or at any rate analogous, to a criminal indifference to consequences" (per Lord Justice-Clerk Aitchison at 22) (but see note on *Transco plc* v *HM Advocate* (2004) below).

HM Advocate v Harris (1993): established that recklessly causing injury is a crime in its own right without any need to allege that the reckless act was to the danger of the lieges.

Robson v Spiers (1999): if the danger which the act causes or will cause is foreseeable, this is enough to establish recklessness.

Cameron v Maguire (1999): "zeroing" a rifle without taking on board the inherent risks amounts to culpably and recklessly endangering the lieges.

Khaliq v HM Advocate (1984): sale of glue-sniffing kits to children is a criminal act (the old crime of causing real injury) because of the accused's knowledge of the ultimate harmful use to which they will be put.

Ulhaq v HM Advocate (1991): sale of glue-sniffing kits is equally causing real injury where the purchasers (and victims) are adults as where they are children.

Transco plc v HM Advocate (2004): subjected the definition of the *mens rea* of recklessness from *Paton* v *HM Advocate* (1936) to some criticism, stating that "gross or wicked indifference to consequences" or "a want of care which is grave" explain the concept better. It also holds that recklessness must be a state of mind, thereby indicating a subjective standard.

10 HOMICIDE

CRIMINAL HOMICIDE: *ACTUS REUS*

There are two crimes of homicide in Scots law: murder and culpable homicide. The behavioural element of both is the same: "the destruction of life" (Macdonald, 89). A homicide charge remains competent no matter how long after the initial attack the death occurs. Conviction of assault *and* homicide arising out of the same incident is, therefore, possible. Thus, murder and culpable homicide are not just forms of aggravated assault but crimes in their own right.

When does life end?

The point at which the victim's life is terminated is a question of fact in each case. In *Finlayson* v *HM Advocate* (1979) it was held that the switching off of a life-support machine did not constitute a *novus actus interveniens* in the chain of causation between the original wrongful act and the death.

When does life begin?

It is only homicide where the life in question is self-existent. This is an issue in relation to babies who suffer injuries in their mothers' wombs. If the baby has lived and breathed unaided, independently of its mother, even for a short time, then a charge of homicide may be relevant.

In *McCluskey* v *HM Advocate* (1989), the charge was causing death by reckless driving, and the victim was a baby still in its mother's womb. It was held that the charge was appropriate because the child had lived outside the womb, even though only for a short period.

SUICIDE

It is not a crime in Scotland to destroy your own life.

MURDER

Since both murder and culpable homicide have the same *actus reus*, it is the *mens rea* which distinguishes them. The distinction matters because conviction of murder carries an automatic life sentence. For culpable homicide, the whole spectrum of sentencing options is available.

Macdonald's is the accepted definition of murder though it has been modified by the decision in *Drury* v *HM Advocate* (2001): "[m]urder is constituted by a wilful act causing the destruction of life, whether [wickedly] intended to kill, or displaying such wicked recklessness as to imply a disposition depraved enough to be regardless of the consequences" (at 89).

Mens rea

From this, it is clear that there are two possible *mens rea* for murder: (1) wicked intention to kill; or (2) wicked recklessness. These are separate and distinct mental elements and only one need be proved.

Intention to kill ("wicked" intention)

Until 2001, all that was necessary to satisfy the "intention" arm of the definition was that the accused intended to kill the victim at the time when the attack took place. The five-judge Bench in the case of *Drury* v *HM Advocate* (2001), however, held that murder required a *wicked* intention to kill. It stated that:

> "just as the recklessness has to be wicked so also must the intention be wicked. Therefore, perhaps the most obvious way of completing the [classic] definition [of murder from Macdonald] is by saying that murder is constituted by any wilful act causing the destruction of life, by which the perpetrator either wickedly intends to kill or displays wicked recklessness as to whether the victim lives or dies" (per Lord Justice-General Rodger at p 1016).

There has been much academic discussion of the decision in *Drury*, including how it might be applied in individual cases. For example, if intention to kill is no longer enough, does this render mercy killing culpable homicide on the basis that, while the killer intends the death, she undertakes the killing for benign reasons? Her intention is not wicked. "Wicked", in this context, has generally been interpreted to mean simply that the accused has no workable defence to the murder charge – but no other crime incorporates possible defences in this way. In short, *Drury* is an anomalous decision which is quite difficult to reconcile with existing principle. Nonetheless, it was decided by a Full Bench of the High Court and is therefore authoritative and binding.

Premeditation

Although it appears that the intention must now be wicked, there is no requirement that the killing be premeditated. This was clarified in *HM Advocate* v *Macdonald* (1867).

"Wicked recklessness"

Wicked recklessness constitutes a separate and alternative *mens rea* for murder, as was determined in the case of *Cawthorne* v *HM Advocate* (1968). In that case, the accused fired a high-velocity rifle into a room where, to his knowledge, four people had retreated to take refuge from him. He made no attempt to mitigate the danger he caused but fired five shots at a height where he might reasonably have been expected to injure someone seriously. It was held that the *mens rea* of murder (or, in this specific case, attempted murder) could be proved by evidence of a deliberate intention to kill *or* by such recklessness as to show that the accused was regardless of the consequences of his actions – in other words, that the accused was completely indifferent as to whether death resulted from his actions.

The High Court gave close consideration to the meaning of wicked recklessness in *HM Advocate* v *Purcell* (2008).

This case concerned a motorist who, during a spree of extremely dangerous driving, killed a 10-year-old boy at a pedestrian crossing in Edinburgh. The Crown sought to charge Purcell with murder. The facts were that the traffic signal was showing a green man for pedestrians, in response to which the victim was crossing. Purcell pulled on to the wrong side of the road to overtake traffic which had stopped in obedience to the red light for vehicles. He then had to make a "chicane" manoeuvre – driving diagonally through the crossing to avoid the cars stopped at the other side. In so doing he knocked down the victim who died of his injuries.

The High Court considered previous authorities on wicked recklessness and concluded that, before there can be a murder conviction, the accused's actions must have been intended to cause some personal injury *as well as* demonstrating utter indifference to fatal consequences. Purcell's actions were not so intended, therefore, only a culpable homicide charge was appropriate.

The recent case of *Petto* v *HM Advocate* (2009) required the High Court to look again at this issue. The accused had stabbed the first victim to death in a ground-floor flat. He pled guilty to culpable homicide in relation to that attack. Immediately after the killing, with a number of co-accused, he had poured a large quantity of petrol throughout the flat and set the building itself (a tenement containing eight flats in total) alight. A resident of another flat died as a result of the fire. Petto initially pled guilty to murder in relation to her death but subsequently appealed on the basis that the charge did not disclose all of the requisite elements of murder, as these had been set down in *Purcell*. In particular, he questioned whether the wilful fireraising of the block of flats could demonstrate the necessary intention to cause personal injury which *Purcell* had required. The High Court suggested that, where it was known that there were other persons in a building who would be affected by the fire, then "the act of wilfully setting fire to a house could ... reasonably be deemed to be an assault on the other occupants of the house" (per Lord Wheatley at 512). The secondary issue was whether the wilful act had to be specifically directed against the ultimate deceased. The court took the view that, provided there was "a clear intention to do physical harm to *someone*, or [the accused had] displayed such gross recklessness as amounts to the same thing" (per Lord Wheatley at 512, emphasis added) that was sufficient. It acknowledged, however, that there was no authority for these views and, accordingly referred the matter to a larger court for fuller consideration.

The law is currently as set out in *Purcell*, then – that there is a need for intention to cause personal injury but *Petto*, when it is heard by the larger Bench, may state it differently. The other strand to wicked recklessness, which will now be considered, is the concept of utter indifference to fatal consequences which it requires.

It is clear from *Halliday* v *HM Advocate* (1999) that the court is looking for a display of utter indifference towards the victim (or "complete, utter and wicked disregard of the consequences of [the] attack on the deceased" (per Lord Justice-General Rodger at 487)). In that case, the appellants had been convicted of murder and the only issue, both at the trial and on appeal, was whether the killing amounted to murder or culpable homicide. The deceased was kicked by the appellants and left motionless. The appellants moved away, shook hands, said what great brothers they were, then returned and kicked the deceased again and stamped on his head. They then put him in the recovery position and went home and washed their clothes. Some time later, they went out to look at the deceased, were unable to find a pulse and called an ambulance.

It was held that the evidence of what happened once the attack was over (the washing of the clothes) could cast light on the attitude of the appellants at the time of the attack. Their actions tended to show that they had been wickedly indifferent to the consequences of the attack. They were accordingly correctly convicted of murder.

Wicked recklessness requires, at base, and colloquially, that the accused could not care less whether the victim lives or dies – that he or she has demonstrated utter indifference as to the victim's life. It is this which differentiates the "*wicked* recklessness" required for murder from recklessness in non-fatal crimes of violence.

Lethal weapons. If the accused uses a lethal weapon in the attack, this is likely to raise the inference that there is a total disregard of the consequences for the victim and that the crime is, therefore, murder. In *HM Advocate* v *McGuinness* (1937), Lord Justice-Clerk Aitchison stated that "[p]eople who use knives and pokers and hatchets against a fellow citizen are not entitled to say 'we did not mean to kill', if death results. If people resort to the use of deadly weapons of this kind, they are guilty of murder, whether or not they intended to kill" (at 40).

This cannot be taken as a blanket pronouncement that, if a lethal weapon is used, the crime is automatically murder. Gordon (para 23.23) points out that the term "deadly weapon" is not helpful because people can be killed by, for example, being kicked to death (as in *Halliday*). *Hopkinson* v *HM Advocate* (2009) demonstrates, for example, in the art and part context, that the use to which the accused thought the weapon would be put can be decisive in determining whether the crime is murder or culpable homicide. The issue is always, therefore "was there wicked recklessness in relation to the particular set of events charged?".

Art and part murder. It should be borne in mind that, in cases of murder by one or more co-accused on an art and part basis where there was a common plan (or pre-concert) the mental element is whether it was "was objectively foreseeable to the [co-accused in question] that such violence was liable to be used as carried an obvious risk of life being taken" (*Poole* v *HM Advocate* (2009) per Lord Kingarth at para 11).

Defences to a murder charge

Self-defence

Self-defence is a complete defence to a charge of murder. If it is successful, the accused is acquitted.

The underlying rationale is that the physical force used by the accused was justifiable to protect him- or herself from an attack by the victim. It is of the essence of self-defence that the accused accepts that they did use the violence alleged against the victim. Accordingly, if the plea is unsuccessful, the accused will be left to face the consequences of their admission in that respect.

There are three essential elements to a plea of self-defence:

(1) Imminent danger to life. In a murder case, self-defence can be pled only when the violence was necessary for either the protection of life or the prevention of rape.

The danger to life must be imminent. Similarly to the defences of coercion and necessity, self-defence is not available where the deceased threatens to use violence in the future. The accused must fear that if he or she does not act immediately, they themselves will be killed.

This was affirmed in the unreported case of *HM Advocate* v *Greig* (1979). The accused killed her husband while he was dozing in a chair. The judge refused to allow the issue of self-defence to go to the jury, because the fact that the husband was sleeping meant that Greig could not have been in imminent fear for her life. This was despite the fact that he had been violent towards her on a number of previous occasions and she stated that she was afraid of what he would do when he woke up.

It is legitimate to use the defence to protect someone else from a life-threatening attack. In *Boyle* v *HM Advocate* (1993), three points were raised and settled. First, an accused who starts a fight is entitled to plead self-defence where appropriate. Second, it is not an absolute bar to the plea that the accused enters the fight armed with a lethal weapon. Finally, the fact that the accused had entered the fight to protect a friend is no bar to the plea. The imminency of the danger to life is the key element. *Dewar* v *HM Advocate* (2009) states that, where the violence is employed in defence of a third party, clear directions must be given to the jury as to how all aspects of the defence apply.

Following *Burns* v *HM Advocate* (1995), the issue of self-defence in a self-induced fight depends on whether the retaliation by the eventual victim was such that the accused was entitled to defend himself.

Error as to imminency of attack. So long as the accused acted in the belief that he was facing imminent, life-threatening violence, the plea of self-defence is available, even if the belief is mistaken. Similarly to theft, the mistaken belief must be based on reasonable grounds.

In *Jones* v *HM Advocate* (1990), the accused alleged that the victim had come to his house earlier on the evening of his death carrying a knife and had threatened him. Accordingly, when he went out later, the accused stated that he had taken a knife with him. He met the victim on the street, pushed him, and walked away. He then felt a knife-prick so he pulled out his own knife and stabbed the deceased on the leg, stabbing him on the chest as he fell to the ground.

It was held that the test for self-defence was whether the appellant believed on reasonable grounds that he was in danger of losing his life. In this case, however, no reasonable jury could have found that there were such grounds. *Lieser* v *HM Advocate* (2008) affirmed the test.

Prevention of rape. Self-defence may also be pled where the accused alleges that he or she has acted to prevent an imminent rape. In the case of *Pollock* v *HM Advocate* (1998), the accused killed another man who, he alleged, had assaulted his (Pollock's) girlfriend with intent to rape her. The court accepted that self-defence could be pled in these circumstances, but the plea was withdrawn from the jury because Pollock had acted with excessive savagery towards the victim.

Self-defence to rape is only applicable as a defence where the alleged victim is a woman. At common law, this is at least in line with principle in that rape victims must be female. S 1 of the Sexual Offences (Scotland) Act 2009, however, defines the crime of rape so as to include penetration of the anus by the penis, thereby including male victims. The impact which this will have, when it is brought into force, on this aspect of self-defence, can currently only be the subject of speculation. The Act does not deal with self-defence. The common law is unequivocal that self-defence does not apply to male rape. This was established in the case of *McCluskey* v *HM Advocate* (1959), where, at first instance, Lord Strachan refused to put the plea to the jury in circumstances where the accused admitted that there had been no threat to his life but only an attempt by the deceased to commit sodomy on him. On appeal, Lord Justice-General Clyde stressed that danger *to life*, not merely to virtue, was a necessary pre-condition of the plea. This view was upheld in *Elliott* v *HM Advocate* (1987). The evidence there indicated that the accused's fear was that he would be subjected to a homosexual attack, not that he was likely to lose his life. Accordingly, his plea of self-defence was not appropriate.

(2) Inability to escape/violence as last resort. The second test which must be satisfied to establish self-defence is the absence of any other reasonable means of escape. If the accused can reasonably escape, he should do so. In the case of *HM Advocate* v *Doherty* (1954), the accused was attacked by another man with a hammer. The accused was with a number of his friends and there was an open door leading down a flight of stairs and into a yard behind him. One of the accused's friends handed him a bayonet and he stabbed the deceased with it. The accused had force on his side and an escape route available had he chosen to use it. Accordingly, he was convicted, as charged, of culpable homicide.

Dewar v *HM Advocate* (2009) decided that this test may not apply, or may apply differently, where the accused used the violence to defend a third party. In *Dewar*, where the charge was assault rather than homicide, the accused alleged that he had stabbed the victim in the back with a pen-knife because, at that point, the victim was sitting on top of the accused's friend and punching him in the face, aiming for his eyes. Clearly, it would have been possible for Dewar himself to escape at that point – he was not being attacked. Nonetheless, the directions given by the trial judge were in the standard terms. This amounted to a miscarriage of justice. The violence must be used as a last resort but the judge must direct the jury by reference to the circumstances in question. By saying that Dewar should have taken any available means of escape, he had failed to do so.

(3) Force used should not be excessive. The force used by the accused should not be cruelly excessive to that used against him by the victim. It must not be greater than what is reasonably necessary to repel the attack. This can be seen in *Pollock* v *HM Advocate* (1998), where the accused acted to save his girlfriend from rape. When the accused arrived at the locus, the deceased had his hand over the accused's girlfriend's mouth. When this was removed the girlfriend shouted that the deceased had been trying to rape her. The accused responded to this by repeatedly stamping on the deceased's head, causing more than 70 injuries. In evidence he alleged that he thought that the deceased had had a knife. His plea of self-defence was rejected on the ground that the force used was far in excess of any danger which he or his girlfriend faced.

Note that the courts take account of the fact that the accused acts in the heat of the moment and they therefore do not weigh the proportionality requirement in "too fine scales" (per Lord Keith in *HM Advocate* v *Doherty* (1954) at 4).

Consent on the part of the victim

It is no defence to a murder charge that the victim consented. In *HM Advocate* v *Rutherford* (1947), the accused killed the victim by strangling her with his tie. He argued that she had asked him to do so and that therefore the killing was an accident which had, in any event, taken place with her consent. Lord Justice-Clerk Cooper dealt with this simply by informing the jury that consent was not a defence to murder – and this seems to have been accepted as a matter of law.

CULPABLE HOMICIDE

Culpable homicide is a "sweep-up" offence. It applies to all cases of killing which are neither accidental nor justifiable, and which are not sufficiently serious to amount to murder. As Lord Justice-General Rodger put it in *Drury* v *HM Advocate* (2001) "the crime of culpable homicide covers the killing of human beings in all circumstances, short of murder, where the criminal law attaches a relevant measure of blame to the person who kills" (at 1017). It is usually divided into three categories:

(1) Voluntary culpable homicide

Voluntary culpable homicide exists where the crime committed might, technically, satisfy the definition of murder but a reason – usually the operation of the defence of provocation or of diminished responsibility – exists making it appropriate, instead, to return a verdict of guilty only of culpable homicide.

Provocation

Provocation is *not* a complete defence. It is often said that it operates to reduce murder to culpable homicide. *Drury* v *HM Advocate* (2001) indicates, however, that, strictly, provocation provides a reason making it more correct to convict of culpable homicide than murder. This is because someone who kills under provocation may fully intend to kill his victim but that intention is not a "wicked" intention. The intention only arises because of the provoking act. Accordingly, the accused does not in fact have the *mens rea* for murder in the first place. His action, although culpable, was not wicked. As Lord Justice-General Rodger explained it in *Drury* (at 1018)

> "While the terminology of 'reducing murder to culpable homicide' is frequently encountered, it is essentially misleading . . . In particular, it suggests that the jury would first conclude that, absent provocation, the accused would have been guilty of murder, and only at that stage would they consider provocation. In reality, however, evidence relating to provocation is simply one of the factors which the jury should take into account in performing their general task of determining the accused's state of mind at the time when he killed his victim."

Provocation is an excuse. The accused's actions are still seen as wrong but they can be partly excused by what happened to him in the first place. The action is still criminal but the law accepts that human frailty will sometimes lead people to lose all control in the face of provocation.

The classic definition of provocation is still that given by Macdonald: "The defence of provocation is of this sort – 'Being agitated and excited and alarmed by violence, I lost control over myself, and took life when my presence of mind had left me, and without thought of what I was doing'" (Macdonald, 135).

There are three requirements for a successful defence of provocation, though the third varies depending upon the nature of the provoking act itself:

(1) Loss of self-control. The loss of self-control is of the essence of the defence of provocation. The case of *Low* v *HM Advocate* (1994) established that there must be some evidence of the loss of self-control. If the trial judge takes the view that there is none, then the defence should not be put to the jury.

In *Drury* v *HM Advocate* (2001), counsel for Drury argued that, if it could be proved that the accused had lost his self-control, that should be enough to establish the defence. If the provocation had been sufficient to cause him to lose his self-control in the first place then, by definition, he had no control and, while provoked, he could not be expected to exercise any restraint. If that view was accepted, all that would require to be proved was that the accused had been subjected to a provoking act and had lost self-control in response to it. The five-judge court rejected this on the basis that it implied, wrongly, that "there [was] no intermediate stage between icy detachment and going berserk" (Lord Justice-General Rodger at 1020 quoting Lord Diplock in *Phillips* v *The Queen* (1969), at 137). Even where there has been a provoking act, individuals still retain some degree of control over their actions.

(2) Provoking acts. Scots law recognises two types of provoking act: (a) an initial assault by the victim; and (b) the discovery of sexual infidelity. Informing an individual verbally of such infidelity is the only circumstance in which words can constitute a provoking act for the purposes of the defence.

In *Cosgrove* v *HM Advocate* (1990), the High Court did state: "[i]t must be remembered that every case depends on its own circumstances and I suppose it is possible that in some situations a judge might leave the question of provocation to the jury even though the evidence does not fit the classic definition in Macdonald but we have no doubt that the classic definition is still the proper direction to give" (per Lord Cowie at 339).

This might suggest a slight weakening of the absoluteness of the position that only assault or the discovery of sexual infidelity will suffice to ground a plea of provocation. In practice, however, the courts appear to be holding resolutely to these traditional requirements. (In *Cosgrove*, the evidence suggested that the deceased had admitted to indecent conduct with a child and had smirked while doing so. This did not amount to provocation.)

Violence. Scots law recognises an initial assault by the victim as a provoking act. A very minor assault is unlikely to "palliate the taking of the deceased's life" (*Thomson* v *HM Advocate* (1986) per Lord Justice-Clerk Ross at 284).

Sexual infidelity. The line of cases establishing that the discovery of sexual infidelity on the part of a partner can constitute a provoking act commenced with *HM Advocate* v *Hill* (1941), where the accused was a corporal in the military police, stationed in England. He arrived home in Springburn because he was suspicious that his wife might have been unfaithful to him. On arrival, he confronted his wife and the other man (a William Headland) and they confirmed that they were having an ongoing sexual relationship. Hill went immediately to get his service revolver and shot dead both his wife and Headland. The trial judge directed the jury that provocation was a valid defence in these circumstances and the accused was convicted only of culpable homicide on that basis.

This principle has now been extended beyond the marital relationship, to any relationship where the court can conclude that it is appropriate for each partner to expect sexual fidelity from the other. In *HM Advocate* v *Callander* (1958), it was accepted that a husband's discovery of his wife's lesbian relationship could ground a plea of provocation. In *McDermott* v *HM Advocate* (1973), the accused was living with a woman and lost his self-control when he discovered that she was having an "illicit association" (per Lord Justice-General Emslie at 11) with the victim. In *HM Advocate* v *McKean* (1997) the judge ruled that infidelity in a lesbian (or, indeed, any homosexual) relationship could provide the basis for a plea of provocation.

The discovery of sexual infidelity was the main issue with which *Drury* v *HM Advocate* (2001) was concerned. Drury had been having an on-off sexual relationship with the deceased and had at one time lived with her for a 16-month period. Although this seems to have been disputed, the court accepted that it was appropriate to infer that, at the time of the attack, the relationship was such that Drury was entitled to expect fidelity from the victim. Drury arrived at her house at about midnight on the night of the attack. He had some difficulty in getting anyone to answer the door. Finally, a blond-haired man ran out, adjusting his clothes and the deceased (Marilyn McKenna) ran out into the street behind him. Drury asked her what the man was doing there and her answer led him to believe that they had been having sex. Drury then grabbed a claw-hammer from a coal bunker at the side of the house and attacked the deceased about the head, inflicting injuries which one of the medical witnesses described as the worst she had ever seen.

The five-judge court affirmed that the plea of provocation was available to an accused in circumstances like Drury's, provided that the expectation of sexual fidelity could be established by the evidence.

(3) An appropriate response. Scots law allows the defence of provocation only where the accused has responded within well-defined parameters to the provoking act. These parameters are different depending on whether the provocation consists of violence or infidelity.

(a) Response to violence. There must be immediate retaliation and "some equivalence between the retaliation and the provocation so that the violence used by the accused is not grossly disproportionate to the evidence constituting the provocation" (*Low* v *HM Advocate* (1994), per Lord Justice-Clerk Ross at 286). In *Gillon* v *HM Advocate* (2006), a five-judge court specially convened for the purpose confirmed that this remains the appropriate test where the provocation is an attack by the deceased.

In *Thomson* v *HM Advocate* (1986), the accused and the deceased had been in business together but had disagreed sharply and were in the process of agreeing severance terms. They met at the business premises so that the accused could remove certain articles which he needed to carry on business as a plumber. The accused was armed with a kitchen knife to protect himself, and to threaten anyone who tried to prevent him removing his equipment.

At the meeting, the accused claimed that the deceased had laughed at him, had reneged on the agreement and had refused to allow the removal of the equipment. The deceased had then pulled the accused back into the office as he was attempting to leave.

The court held that, far from establishing evidence of provocation, the history of increasingly embittered relations between the accused and the deceased provided the accused with a motive for murder. More specifically, any violence in response to the course of dealings would not satisfy the test of immediate retaliation. It was possible that the deceased's final act in pulling the accused could constitute a provoking act. In this case, however, the accused's response to that – he stabbed the deceased 11 times with the kitchen knife – was grossly disproportionate to the provocation itself and the defence therefore failed.

(b) Response to discovery of sexual infidelity. In *Drury* v *HM Advocate* (2001), the five-judge court expressly rejected an argument by the Crown that the violence offered in response to the discovery of infidelity had to be proportionate to the provocation. This, it said, could not be the case because there was no mechanism for measuring the two responses against each other in any meaningful way. Instead, it said that the appropriate question for the court to ask was whether the accused had over-reacted to the provocation in the way in which an ordinary man or woman would have done. If so, the law would recognise him as weak rather than wicked and the defence of provocation would succeed. If, however, the accused over-reacts in a way which is not ordinary, the jury is entitled to conclude that he acted with the necessary wickedness to justify a conviction for murder.

General immediacy requirement. Whether the provoking act is violence or the discovery of sexual infidelity, it appears that the accused must respond immediately to it. The fact that the accused's use of fatal violence against his business partner in *Thomson* v *HM Advocate* (1986) was partly in response to a pre-existing course of business dealings meant that it was not an immediate response. This was one reason for the failure of the partial defence of provocation.

Diminished responsibility

The other defence which operates in the same way as provocation is diminished responsibility. Where it is pled successfully, it will have the effect of reducing a murder charge to culpable homicide. Unlike provocation, however, the onus of proving diminished responsibility is placed on the accused on the balance of probabilities. This procedural requirement was clarified in the case of *Lindsay* v *HM Advocate* (1997).

Diminished responsibility arises where the accused suffers from some mental abnormality which impairs his or her ability to decide on and control their actions. The most important case in this area is *Galbraith* v *HM Advocate* (2002).

The crime took place in Furnace, a small village in Argyll. The accused shot dead her husband, who was a police officer, using one of his own rifles. She then took various steps to suggest that two intruders had broken in, and made a 999 call to the police, claiming that that was what had happened.

At the trial for murder, the defence of diminished responsibility was rejected and Galbraith's appeal against conviction turned, effectively, on whether the trial court had correctly understood and applied the law on diminished responsibility. The issue was referred to a five-judge court which decided that the pre-existing interpretation of the law (which had been applied in Galbraith's trial) had been flawed and excessively restrictive. Accordingly, *Galbraith* broadens out the definition of diminished responsibility.

The accused now needs to prove that he or she was suffering from some "mental abnormality" such that their ability to determine and control their actings, as compared with that of a "normal" person, was substantially impaired. This is a legal test. Although evidence from medical witnesses and/or psychologists may be required, it is ultimately a question for the judge. He must decide whether, in law, that evidence discloses a basis on which the accused's responsibility for their actions could be regarded as diminished. If not, then it is not appropriate to put the issue of diminished responsibility to the jury at all.

"Mental abnormality". The five-judge court in *Galbraith* gave general guidance as to the meaning of the term "mental abnormality". As examples, it suggested that (1) the accused might perceive physical acts and matters differently from a normal person; or (2) it might affect the accused's ability to form a rational judgment as to whether a particular act was right or wrong or as to whether to perform that act.

Following previous decisions of the High Court, *Galbraith* affirmed that neither self-induced impairment, through the ingestion of alcohol or drugs (*Brennan* v *HM Advocate* (1977)), nor psychopathic personality disorder (*Carraher* v *HM Advocate* (1946)) could ground a plea of diminished responsibility.

In *Galbraith*, the accused's claim of "mental abnormality", although it was not specifically couched in those terms, arose from the violence, both physical and sexual, which she alleged that the deceased had used towards her over a number of years. It is arguable, therefore, that the door has been opened to a defence based on "battered woman syndrome".

Similarly to insanity, diminished responsibility is covered by the Criminal Justice and Licensing (Scotland) Bill ("CJL(S)B") which will, assuming it is enacted in its current form, place it on a statutory footing. It is necessary to examine the Bill's provisions.

Diminished responsibility will continue to be applicable only in relation to murder. The onus of proof will remain on the accused on the balance of probabilities (CJL(S)B, s 117, inserting a new s 51B(4) into the Criminal Procedure (Scotland) Act 1995). The effect of a successful plea will be that "[a] person who would otherwise be convicted of murder is instead to be convicted of culpable homicide" (CJL(S)B, s 117, inserting a new s 51B(1) into the Criminal Procedure (Scotland) Act 1995).

The statutory test will be met "if the person's ability to determine or control conduct [which includes acts and omissions] for which the person would otherwise be convicted of murder was, at the time of the conduct, substantially impaired by reason of abnormality of mind" (CJL(S)B, s 117, inserting a new s 51B(1) into the Criminal Procedure (Scotland) Act 1995).

In terms of the Bill, the effect of being under the influence of alcohol, drugs or any other substance at the time of the killing would be neutral. It would neither automatically constitute abnormality of mind nor would it prevent this from being established (CJL(S)B s 117, inserting a new s 51B(3) into the Criminal Procedure (Scotland) Act 1995). Since the Bill makes no reference at all to psychopathic personality disorder in relation to diminished responsibility, such a condition could form the basis of this plea if its effects meant that the accused met the statutory test.

(2) Involuntary culpable homicide

In Scots criminal law, there are two forms of *involuntary* culpable homicide – where culpable homicide is seen as a crime in its own right and not as mitigated murder:

(a) Unintentional culpable homicide in the course of an unlawful act or involuntary unlawful act culpable homicide

This first, "unlawful act", type arises where the accused is engaged in committing a crime and, through his or her criminal actions, causes someone else's death, though the death itself is unintentional. It is no longer the law that, if the accused is involved in any criminal enterprise whatsoever, and death results to a victim, the crime then becomes involuntary unlawful act culpable homicide. Only certain crimes can form the basis of this type of culpable homicide. The *actus reus* of this form of culpable homicide is, as with all homicide in Scots law, the destruction of life. The *mens rea* is the *mens rea* for the underlying crime – the crime in which the accused was engaged from which the death resulted. It is not, however, clear to which crimes other than assault this principle now applies.

Assault cases. It is clear, for obvious reasons, that assault can underlie involuntary unlawful act culpable homicide, because the accused is required to take responsibility for all the consequences of his or her action and to take the victim as they find him. Thus, where the Crown can prove the assault *and* that the assault has caused the death then the accused will be convicted of this type of culpable homicide. The relevant *mens rea* is that of assault. The only other issue is whether the accused demonstrated the *mens rea* for murder – either wicked recklessness or a wicked intention to kill. If so, then murder will be the appropriate charge.

Death arising in the course of other crimes. It is unclear if there is any crime, other than assault, which would automatically incur a culpable homicide charge where the victim dies. Gordon's view is that it might be applicable to fireraising offences "because of the dangerous nature of the crime and the consequent very high duty to take care not to injure anyone" (Gordon para 26-27, footnote 53). Certainly, in *Mathieson* v *HM Advocate* (1981), the underlying crime was culpable and reckless fireraising.

The matter has been considered very recently in the case of *MacAngus and Kane* v *HM Advocate* (2009). This case affirms the view that this (unlawful act) form of culpable homicide will be limited to those crimes (such as "assault or analogous cases" (per Lord Justice-General Hamilton at para 29)) where the accused's actions can be seen as being directed against the deceased.

(b) Unintentional culpable homicide in the course of a lawful act or involuntary lawful act culpable homicide

In involuntary *lawful* act culpable homicide, the accused will have caused the death while engaged in an activity which is otherwise lawful. This type of culpable homicide therefore carries with it its own *mens rea*: recklessness on the *Paton* v *HM Advocate* (1936) model of "gross, or wicked, or criminal negligence, something amounting, or at any rate analogous, to a criminal indifference to consequences" (per Lord Justice-Clerk Aitchison at 22) (though subject to the caveats arising from the case of *Transco plc* v *HM Advocate* (2004) discussed in Chapter 9).

The judgment in *Transco* also clarifies that a state of mind is required, rather than an objective assessment of whether the accused's *behaviour* falls below the standard expected. The question is not "Did the accused act recklessly?" but, rather, "Did he possess the necessary state of mind alongside the action causing death?" (and see the discussion in Chapter 9).

This category is perhaps the most confusing. It clearly arises where the accused's initial activity is lawful. It is also used, however, where the accused is engaged in an unlawful activity but the *unlawful* act category is not deemed appropriate because the accused did not intend any physical harm, nor were his actions directed against the deceased.

This can be seen from the case of *Sutherland* v *HM Advocate* (1994) in which an individual was killed as he set fire to Mr Sutherland's house. He had been employed by Mr Sutherland to do so for the purpose of making a fraudulent insurance claim. At the trial, the Crown tried to argue that this fell into the *unlawful* act category but the trial judge would not allow this. He held that, although fireraising to defraud insurers is a crime, it is not a relevant crime for the purposes of the *unlawful* act category. It does not involve behaviour directed against the deceased nor an intention to do him physical harm. Accordingly, the Crown had to prove that the accused acted with the requisite degree of recklessness and that his reckless actions actually caused the death.

This accords with the decision in *MacAngus and Kane* v *HM Advocate* (2009) where a five-judge Bench was convened. In *Khaliq* v *HM Advocate* (1984), the charge (of causing real injury) related to the supply by the accused of glue-sniffing kits to children. There was no allegation that the accused had *administered* the solvent fumes. The High Court held that the mere fact that the purchasers of the kits had to do something themselves – ie inhale the fumes – before harm would result did not break the chain of causation between the accused's act and that harm. If the accused's knowledge of the potential harm could be made out, he was culpable. This had been taken to its natural conclusion in the *Lord Advocate's Reference (No 1 of 1994)* (1996) where the accused's friend (who was, ultimately, the deceased) had asked him to obtain some of the drug, Ecstasy. He did this and handed it over to her. She divided it up between herself and a number of other friends and decided exactly which dose she would take herself. This ultimately proved fatal. It was held that this did amount to the crime of culpable homicide because the supply was the equivalent of culpable and reckless conduct and the accused knew that the drug was potentially harmful.

In *MacAngus and Kane* v *HM Advocate* (2009), the High Court was called upon to reconsider this issue. It took the view that where a, potentially harmful, substance (in *MacAngus*, the substances were ketamine and, separately in another charge, heroin) was supplied, *and the Crown could establish recklessness in relation to that supply*, then the deceased's intervention, in taking the drug consensually, did not necessarily break the chain of causation. Accordingly, it appears that culpable homicide arising in such circumstances effectively belongs to the lawful act category in that it cannot be made out without proof of recklessness.

Essential Facts

- When life ends is a question of fact in every individual case.
- A life must be self-existent before any question of homicide can arise.
- The *actus reus* of both forms of criminal homicide – murder and culpable homicide – is "the destruction of life" (Macdonald, 89).
- Suicide is not a crime in Scots law.
- Murder and culpable homicide are distinguishable only by their *mens rea*.
- There are two possible, alternative *mens rea* for murder: wicked intention to kill and wicked recklessness.
- Wicked recklessness requires an intention to cause personal injury together with utter indifference on the part of the accused towards the victim as to whether he or she lives or dies. The use of a lethal weapon in the attack is likely to raise an inference that this *mens rea* is satisfied, but is not conclusive of the point.
- In art and part murder cases, where there was a common plan (or pre-concert) the mental element is whether it was was objectively foreseeable to the co-accused in question that such violence was liable to be used as carried an obvious risk of life being taken.
- Self-defence is a complete defence to a charge of murder (and, indeed, assault). It can be pled where the violence was necessary either for the protection of life or for the prevention of rape. Currently, it cannot be used, at common law, to prevent so-called "male rape".

- The requirements of self-defence are: (1) imminent danger to life (either the accused's own or that of a third party); (2) no other reasonable means of escape (or that the accused's violence should be offered as a last resort); and (3) that the force used should not be cruelly excessive to that offered by the deceased.

- If the accused's belief that his life is in danger is erroneous, it may still ground a plea of self-defence, provided that it is held on reasonable grounds.

- The victim's consent is no defence to a murder charge.

- Scots law recognises three types of culpable homicide: voluntary culpable homicide; involuntary unlawful act culpable homicide; and involuntary lawful act culpable homicide.

- Voluntary culpable homicide may be regarded as murder "reduced" to culpable homicide, although this is an oversimplification. It arises most commonly where the accused pleads provocation or diminished responsibility to a murder charge.

- Provocation is not a complete defence. Where it is pled successfully, the accused will be convicted of culpable homicide rather than murder. The onus of proof remains on the Crown throughout.

- To establish provocation, there must be evidence of a loss of self-control brought about by a provoking act. The only such acts recognised in Scots law are either an assault by the ultimate victim or the discovery of sexual infidelity. Except where informing of infidelity, words are not sufficient. In the case of either of the accepted forms of provoking act, the accused's response must be immediate. Where the provoking act is violence by the victim, the accused's response must not be grossly disproportionate to the initial violence. Where the provoking act is the discovery of sexual infidelity, the accused's over-reaction to the provocation must have been that of an ordinary man or woman. If it is more extreme, the defence will fail.

- Diminished responsibility can only be pled in relation to a charge of murder. It is not a complete defence but reduces the crime from murder to culpable homicide.

- To establish diminished responsibility, the accused needs to prove that she was suffering from some "mental abnormality" such that her ability to determine and control her actings, as compared with that of a "normal" person, was substantially impaired. This is a legal test. The onus of proof is on the accused on the balance of probabilities.

- Neither self-induced intoxication nor psychopathic personality disorder can ground a plea of diminished responsibility at common law. In terms of the Criminal Justice and Licensing (Scotland) Bill ("CJL(S)B"), once it is enacted, the accused would need to prove himself, on the balance of probabilities, that his ability to determine or control conduct (which includes acts and omissions) for which he would otherwise be convicted of murder was, at the time of the conduct, substantially impaired by reason of abnormality of mind. Self-induced intoxication would be neutral in its effect on the accused's ability to establish diminished responsibility. Psychopathic personality disorder would not be excluded as a basis for the plea.

- Involuntary unlawful act culpable homicide arises where the accused is involved in a criminal enterprise and death results, in circumstances where the *mens rea* for murder is absent. The *actus reus* is the destruction of life; the *mens rea* is the *mens rea* for the underlying crime. The Crown must also prove that the accused's act caused the death.

- Not all crimes can ground involuntary unlawful act culpable homicide. It is limited to those crimes, particularly assault, where the accused's actions can be seen as being directed against the deceased.

- The *mens rea* of involuntary lawful act culpable homicide is recklessness as defined in *Paton* v *HM Advocate* (1936) and refined in *Transco plc* v *HM Advocate* (2004). This category applies not only in circumstances where the act causing death was lawful but also where it was criminal but not directed against the deceased.

Essential Cases

Drury v HM Advocate (2001): the intention to kill must be wicked to satisfy the *mens rea* of murder. In provocation, where the accused was provoked by the discovery of sexual infidelity, his over-reaction to that provocation must be that of an ordinary person. If it is more extreme, he will be convicted of murder.

Cawthorne v HM Advocate (1968): in relation to attempted murder (and murder) wicked recklessness is an alternative *mens rea* to wicked intention to kill.

HM Advocate v Purcell (2008): wicked recklessness requires an intention to cause personal injury together with a wicked disregard of fatal conseqences.

Petto v HM Advocate (2009): considers (but has not yet decided) whether an act (in this case wilful fireraising) which was not directly intended to cause personal injury to the deceased can ground a murder charge following *Purcell*.

Halliday v HM Advocate (1999): a good example of the "wicked disregard of fatal consequences" strand of wicked recklessness.

Boyle v HM Advocate (1993): where self-defence is pled, the imminency of the danger to life is the key element. An accused who starts a fight is entitled to plead self-defence, where appropriate. It is not an absolute bar to the plea that the accused enters the fight armed with a lethal weapon. Self-defence may be pled where the accused entered the fight in order to protect a companion.

Dewar v HM Advocate (2009): in self-defence, where the violence is used in defence of a third party, the "no other reasonable means of escape" test is not appropriate but, rather, the violence should be used as a last resort.

Jones v HM Advocate (1990): if an accused makes an error as to the imminence of danger to his life, he may still be able to use the plea of self-defence, provided that his belief in the danger was held on reasonable grounds.

Lieser v HM Advocate (2008): affirms the position about error in self-defence as set down in *Jones*.

McCluskey v HM Advocate (1959): self-defence may not be used, at least currently, at common law, to prevent so-called "male rape".

HM Advocate v Doherty (1954): if the accused could reasonably escape from the violence offered by the deceased, he must do so. If he does not, the plea of self-defence will fail.

Pollock v HM Advocate (1998): self-defence may be pled where the violence used was for the prevention of rape; however, if it is cruelly excessive to that offered by the deceased, the defence will fail.

HM Advocate v Rutherford (1947): the victim's consent is not a defence to murder.

Low v HM Advocate (1994): to establish provocation, some evidence must be led of the accused's loss of self-control.

HM Advocate v Hill (1941): establishes that the discovery of sexual infidelity can constitute a provoking act for the purposes of provocation.

Gillon v HM Advocate (2006): where the provocation offered is an assault by the deceased, the violence offered in return by the accused must not be grossly disproportionate.

Thomson v HM Advocate (1986): there must be a final provoking act which causes the accused immediatley to lose his self-control and his response to this must not be grossly disproportionate.

Lindsay v HM Advocate (1997): the onus of proving diminished responsibility rests on the accused, on the balance of probabilities.

Galbraith v HM Advocate (2002): diminished responsibility requires that the accused should be suffering from some mental abnormality such that his or her ability to determine and control their actions, as compared with that of a "normal" person, is substantially impaired.

Transco plc v HM Advocate (2004): discussion of the principles of involuntary lawful act culpable homicide. In particular, the case identifies difficulties arising from the definition of recklessness in *Paton* v *HM Advocate* (1936) which is rather circular and clarifies that it is the accused's state of mind which is relevant to establishing *mens rea* – not the way in which he acted.

Sutherland v HM Advocate (1994): although the accused was in the course of committing the crime of fireraising to defraud insurers, as a result of which the victim died, the court held that this was involuntary *lawful* act culpable homicide because the criminal act was not directed against the victim and there was no intention to cause him physical harm.

MacAngus and Kane v HM Advocate (2009): death resulting from the supply of illegal drugs can only constitute involuntary *lawful* act culpable homicide, in that the Crown must prove recklessness. Simple supply from which death results is not sufficient. The deceased's autonomous action in ingesting the drug supplied by the accused does not necessarily break the chain of the causation between the supply and the death.

11 CRIMES AGAINST PUBLIC ORDER

BREACH OF THE PEACE

Breach of the peace has embraced a wide variety of different types of conduct, including walking in the red light district of Aberdeen while dressed as a woman (though being male) (*Stewart* v *Lockhart* (1991)); executing handbrake turns in a car, late at night (*Horsburgh* v *Russell* (1994)); and ordering an Orange Order band to continue playing as it passed a Catholic church as a service was about to start (*McAvoy* v *Jessop* (1989)).

Human rights challenges

In recent years, two cases which raise human rights issues arising from the crime of breach of the peace (*Smith* v *Donnelly* (2002) and *Jones* v *Carnegie* (2004)) have been referred to the High Court. In answering the human rights questions, the High Court also clarified the basic principles of the domestic law in this area.

In *Smith* v *Donnelly* (2002), the accused had been protesting against nuclear weapons. She had lain down on the road and refused to move when asked. She was convicted of breach of the peace at first instance and appealed on the basis that, as a crime, breach of the peace had become so all-encompassing that it could cover virtually any behaviour. She argued that this meant that it was impossible to know in advance of court proceedings whether any act would constitute a breach of the peace. Her case was that this situation was incompatible with Art 7 of the European Convention on Human Rights which requires not only that states should not make criminal law retrospectively, but also that crimes should be sufficiently defined so that individuals can know what acts are criminal at the time when they carry them out. The High Court held that, while the facts of individual breach of the peace cases were disparate, it was possible to derive a core definition of breach of the peace from the leading cases. This was definite enough to satisfy the requirements of Art 7. These core principles will be examined subsequently.

Jones v *Carnegie* (2004) referred five separate appeals on breach of the peace charges from different sheriff courts to a five-judge bench of the High Court. One of its main findings was that *Smith* v *Donnelly* (2002) had been correctly decided on the Art 7 point. In dealing with the appeal of another nuclear protester, who had disrupted proceedings at the Scottish Parliament, the court considered her claim that her Art 10 right to freedom of expression and her Art 11 right to freedom of peaceful assembly and to freedom of association with others had been breached. While it was accepted that removing her from the Parliament building (she had had to be removed bodily from the public gallery) did *interfere* with these rights, the High Court held that the actions of the authorities came within the exceptions to the basic Art 10 and 11 rights set down in Arts 10(2) and 11(2) respectively.

Actus reus

In *Smith* v *Donnelly* (2002), in order to find compatibility with Art 7, the High Court transcended the widely varying facts of individual breach of the peace cases and set down the core principles of breach of the peace, based on *dicta* in three earlier leading cases (the third of which, *Young* v *Heatly* (1959), was subsequently overruled). The first of these was *Ferguson* v *Carnochan* (1889), where the accused had used bad language and oaths and imprecations, which could be heard in the street, early on a Sunday morning. In that case, Lord Justice-Clerk Macdonald drew attention to the essentially objective nature of the crime in that the conduct has to be such as will *reasonably* produce alarm in the minds of the lieges. The test is not, and never has been, whether the individual complainer was actually alarmed.

This point was expanded upon in *Donaldson* v *Vannet* (1998) where the accused had been begging in the street. His conviction for breach of the peace was quashed on appeal, despite the fact that there was evidence that some of the people he approached for money had, in fact, been alarmed by his conduct. The High Court noted that such evidence could not be conclusive in a breach of the peace case "since the subjective reactions of the alleged victims may vary according to their temperament and are thus merely indicators" (per Lord Johnston at 959).

The second case considered by the High Court was *Raffaelli* v *Heatly* (1949). The facts were that the accused had "peeped" in a chink in the curtains in the lighted window of a dwelling house at close to midnight one evening. Lord Justice-Clerk Thomson stated that a breach of the peace occurred "where something is done in breach of public order or decorum which might reasonably be expected to lead to the lieges being alarmed or upset or tempted to make reprisals at their own hand" (at 104).

Finally, the court considered the authorities on the position where there were no witnesses who were *actually* alarmed or annoyed by the conduct, taking the view that provided the conduct in question was "flagrant" (per Lord Coulsfield at para 18) the crime could be established.

However, the more recent case of *Dyer* v *Hutchison* (2006) has restricted the importance to be attached to the word "flagrant". In the context of three separate breach of the peace cases brought in relation to offensive remarks and gestures made at football matches, the High Court stated that, instead of considering whether the relevant conduct was flagrant

> "it is likely to be more helpful to have regard to the whole circumstances surrounding the behaviour complained of in order to determine whether or not it amounts to a breach of the peace ... But, even in the most basic cases of breach of the peace, where there is no evidence of actual distress or alarm, it is well accepted that the question which must be asked is: Would this conduct have been likely to cause distress or alarm to a reasonable person in the vicinity?" (per temporary judge CGB Nicholson at paras [25] and [30]).

Flagrance, then, appears no longer to be the key issue where there is no evidence of actual alarm or distress. It is the likelihood of this being caused to reasonable people in the vicinity which must guide the matter now.

So, what is the current definition of breach of the peace? In *Smith* v *Donnelly* (2002), Lord Coulsfield stated that, in the view of the High Court, it is "clear that what is required to constitute the crime is conduct severe enough to cause alarm to ordinary people and threaten serious disturbance to the community" (at para 17). In *Paterson* v *HM Advocate* (2008), the High Court emphasised that both parts of this test have to be satisfied. In other words, the conduct has to meet both the "severe enough to cause alarm to ordinary people" test and the "threatening serious disturbance to the community test". Satisfying one or the other of these is not sufficient.

Returning to *Smith* v *Donnelly*, Lord Coulsfield went on to state that "[w]hat is required, therefore, ... is conduct which does present as genuinely alarming and disturbing, in its context, to any reasonable person" (at para 17).

Finally, with regard to the definition of breach of the peace generally, *Smith* v *Donnelly* (2002) lists three situations which, unless additional elements or circumstances are also alleged, are now unlikely to be accepted as the basis of a breach of the peace charge on their own. These are: (1) the use of bad language by itself; (2) a failure to co-operate with police officers or other officials, even if forcefully stated; and (3) the disgusting character of words spoken, unless they are accompanied by a real risk of the peace being breached.

The most recent five-judge decision on breach of the peace is *Harris* v *HM Advocate* (2009). The facts were that, in the course of being interviewed on two separate occasions, by two separate police officers, Harris made statements which could have been construed as threatening and which were alleged to have placed each police officer in a state of fear and alarm. Whilst being interviewed at the police station in Dundee, the accused told an inspector that he had engaged a private investigator to find out information about the police officer. Accordingly he now knew where he lived; where his mother lived and details of a mortgage application. The other incident took place during an interview conducted by a police constable over the phone where the accused stated that he had similar personal information including material pertaining to the police officer's brother and the rugby team for which he played. He specifically warned the constable to stay away from him (the accused) and his bank manager.

The real issue here was whether this could possibly constitute a breach of the peace at all. The High Court held that it could not. It reiterated the need for the satisfaction of both strands of the *Smith* v *Donnelly* test. Thus, the fact that conduct is genuinely alarming or disturbing in its context is not sufficient on its own. It is imperative that it also "threatens serious disturbance to the community." In other words, a public element is of the essence of the crime of breach of the peace. The behaviour here took place in private and specifically did not give rise to any risk of members of the public (which here would have consisted of police officers) taking the law into their own hands. The court said that the behaviour in *Harris* was not necessarily not criminal. It might have amounted to the crime of attempting to pervert the course of justice or the common law crime of issuing threats. Nonetheless, it was certainly not breach of the peace. The case of *Young* v *Heatly* (1959), which had held that conduct carried out in private did constitute a breach of the peace, was specifically overruled.

One further point is important. The crime can be constituted where the issue is that the accused's conduct is likely to provoke reprisals from other parties, thus causing a breaking of the social peace at their hand. This can be seen in the case of *Duffield and Crosbie* v *Skeen* (1981) where the co-accused were convicted of breach of the peace after shouting pro-IRA slogans (at 69) at a Celtic football match, and handing out supporting literature. The concern seems to have been more that those who were "disgusted with such slogans" would themselves breach the peace in response. A similar view applies to *Stewart* v *Lockhart* (1991) – the case of the transvestite in the red-light district in Aberdeen mentioned above – and to *Alexander* v *Smith* (1984). In the last case, the accused was selling a National Front newspaper outside Tynecastle football ground in Edinburgh. There was evidence that people attending the football match were annoyed by this.

Mens rea

The *mens rea* of breach of the peace is much neglected in the case law. The basic principle is, however, that common law crimes will have a *mens rea* element. It is important, therefore, to give some consideration to what this might be. There is no requirement that the accused should *intend* to commit a breach of the peace.

In *Ralston* v *HM Advocate* (1989), the accused, a remand prisoner in Barlinnie Prison, was convicted of breach of the peace, at first instance, in relation to a roof-top protest which he undertook in order to draw attention to the poor conditions in which he was being held. He appealed on the basis that his purpose in carrying out the protest had been entirely blameless and that the sheriff, through his directions, had effectively prevented any discussion of the *mens rea* for breach of the peace. Predictably, on appeal, the High Court held that his motives in carrying out the protest were irrelevant. Lord Justice-Clerk Ross said: "whatever his reason was for taking the action which he did, the question for the jury was whether his conduct amounted to disorderly conduct or conduct calculated to cause alarm or annoyance, and thus constituted a breach of the peace. There was no doubt that the appellant's behaviour was deliberate" (at 476).

In *Butcher* v *Jessop* (1989), the breach of the peace took place on the football pitch during a match between Celtic and Rangers. There was an incident in which the Rangers goalkeeper struck a Celtic player (Frank McAvennie) and pushed him to the ground. Terry Butcher, the Rangers captain, also pushed McAvennie. The court endorsed a view, expressed in the 2nd edition of Gordon (para 41-09), that there is no need for the Crown to prove intention to cause a disturbance; all it need establish is that the conduct was "objectively calculated" to do so (at 64). Here, there was no doubt that Butcher's conduct was deliberate and he must also have been aware of the intense rivalry, sometimes turning to animosity between the two groups of fans at the match. His conduct "might reasonably be expected to lead to spectators being alarmed or upset or resorting to violent behaviour" (per Lord Justice-Clerk Ross at 65).

Finally, in *Hughes* v *Crowe* (1993), the accused played loud music and made loud banging noises in his flat between 7.15 and 8.15 on a Saturday morning, causing considerable disturbance to the occupants of the flat below. The court seems to have taken the view that the accused must have been aware that that type of behaviour, at that time on a weekend day, would adversely affect other occupants. There was, however, no evidence that the accused actually knew that the other flat was occupied.

Taken together, then, these cases seem to suggest that the *mens rea* of breach of the peace is deliberate conduct with some degree of awareness of the context in which it is taking place (since it is often that context which turns particular behaviour into a breach of the peace) and, hence, the likely effects.

MOBBING

The crime of mobbing is committed where a number of people come together with a common criminal purpose which they bring about, through sheer force of numbers, by violence and/or intimidation, in the process breaching the peace and causing alarm to the lieges. It does not matter whether or not the ultimate end which they pursue is lawful; if they have a common criminal purpose in the way in which they bring it about, that will still constitute mobbing. In the case of *Kilpatrick* v *HM Advocate* (1992), the co-accused were charged, *inter alia*, with mobbing, after a prison riot. The jury appear to have been satisfied that the two co-accused with whom the case report is concerned "formed part of a mob of evilly disposed persons which conducted itself in a violent, riotous and tumultuous manner, to the great terror and alarm of the lieges and in breach of the peace" (per Lord Justice-General Hope at 123). However, it specifically deleted the part of the charge which alleged that they had had a common criminal purpose. This was held to be fatal to a charge of mobbing. If there is no common criminal purpose, the crime cannot be made out.

The common criminal purpose may either be preconceived or arise spontaneously. However, in either case, that purpose may change as the mob proceeds with the criminal enterprise. Mobbing is a crime in its own right but the individual members of a mob may also be convicted of other crimes committed by the mob if these formed part of the mob's common criminal purpose, at a time when a particular co-accused was acting in furtherance of that common purpose. This presents particular difficulties where the prosecution seeks to secure a conviction of a specific crime (such as murder) on the basis solely that the accused was a member of a mob which committed that crime. In both *Hancock* v *HM Advocate* (1981) and *Coleman* v *HM Advocate* (1999) the High Court was critical of the use of a charge of mobbing because of the additional onus which it placed to prove that, at the time of the specific offence, the accused was a member of the mob, acting in pursuance of its common purpose in a situation where it was foreseeable to him that the mob might commit the other crime. In *Hancock*, all convictions against the co-accused had to be quashed on all charges, because of the failure of the mobbing charge, even though there was clear evidence that a number of individuals had committed discrete offences. Even where the charge is mobbing alone, it is not enough to follow a mob or to be swept along with it. It must be proved that an accused shared its common criminal purpose or "countenanced" its actions.

Scots law specifies no minimum number of persons necessary to constitute a mob. The matter was alluded to in *Sloan* v *Macmillan* (1922), where three co-accused were eventually charged with being part of a "riotous mob" (at 1). A total of 17 people had gone to a mine in the early hours of the morning, during a miners' strike. Their purpose was to intimidate (so that they would stop working) the small staff of volunteers who were keeping the mine in an operational condition during the strike. Only four of the accused actually entered the mine and three of those people appealed their initial conviction of mobbing. The court took the view that the number of people required to constitute a mob depended as much on what they did as their number. It is inferred, however, that the three appellants were always acting along with the 13 others who remained outside. The mobbing conviction was upheld.

Essential Facts

- Breach of the peace consists in conduct which is sufficiently severe to cause alarm to ordinary people *and* to threaten serious disturbance to the community. Both strands of this test must be met. The conduct must be considered in its context and must present as genuinely alarming and disturbing to a reasonable person.

- The test is objective. It does not matter whether the accused considered the conduct to be alarming or disturbing to the social peace but whether a reasonable person would have thought so.

- The *mens rea* is vague but the few cases which consider it can be taken to indicate that the conduct must be carried out deliberately and with awareness of its likely effects in its context.

- The crime may be charged where the accused's conduct is not, *per se*, alarming or threatening but is likely to provoke reprisals.

- No evidence of actual fear or alarm is required but, if there is none, the question which must be asked is: Would this conduct have been likely to cause distress or alarm to a reasonable person in the vicinity?

- A public element is of the essence of breach of the peace.

- Breach of the peace is sufficiently clearly defined to satisfy Art 7 of the European Convention on Human Rights (no punishment without law).

- Mobbing is the coming together of a number of people for a common criminal purpose which they bring about, through sheer force of numbers, by violence and/or intimidation, in the process breaching the peace and alarming the lieges.

- There is no minimum number of members of a mob. It is the nature of their actions which is decisive.

- Mere presence in a mob is not sufficient for a conviction of mobbing. It must be proved that the accused countenanced its criminal purpose.

- Mobbing is a crime in its own right but a mob may commit other crimes as well. To obtain a conviction of such a crime against an individual member of the mob, it must be established that he was, at the time, a member of the mob, participating in its common purpose or that the crime in question was foreseeable to him as a likely outcome of the mob's purpose.

Essential Cases

Smith v Donnelly (2002): defines breach of the peace as "conduct severe enough to cause alarm to ordinary people and threaten serious disturbance to the community ... [or] conduct which does present as genuinely alarming and disturbing, in its context, to any reasonable person". This definition is sufficiently clear not to breach Art 7 of the European Convention on Human Rights (no punishment without law).

Paterson v HM Advocate (2008): the test set down in *Smith* v *Donnelly* (2001) is conjunctive. Both parts must be satisfied.

Jones v Carnegie (2004): a five-judge decision which affirms the view of the law taken in *Smith* v *Donnelly* (2002) and examines, in the context of the facts of the appeals which it decides, the position of Arts 10 and 11.

Ferguson v Carnochan (1889): the test for breach of the peace is an objective one – whether the accused's conduct will reasonably generate alarm in the minds of the lieges.

Raffaelli v Heatly (1949): breach of the peace arises where public order or decorum is breached in a way which might reasonably be expected to alarm or upset the lieges or to tempt them "to make reprisals at their own hand".

Dyer v Hutchison (2006): where there is no evidence of actual alarm or distress, the question which must be asked is: Would this conduct have been likely to cause distress or alarm to a reasonable person in the vicinity?

Harris v HM Advocate (2009): A public element is of the essence of breach of the peace.

Ralston v HM Advocate (1989): the accused's motive in carrying out the conduct is irrelevant. In relation to *mens rea*, the conduct should be carried out deliberately and in a manner calculated to cause alarm or annoyance.

Butcher v Jessop (1989): the *mens rea* of breach of the peace does not require intention to cause a disturbance – merely that the behaviour was "objectively calculated to do so". The accused will have an awareness of the consequences of his actions in the context in which he carries them out.

Hughes v Crowe (1993): in the context of *mens rea*, the court imputed to the accused an awareness of the likely effects of his actions.

Kilpatrick v HM Advocate (1992): if a mob has no common criminal purpose, a charge of mobbing cannot be made out.

Hancock v HM Advocate (1981): where members of the mob are charged with specific offences by virtue of their membership of the mob, the need to prove their acceptance of, and participation in, the mob's common criminal purpose in committing the separate offences may over-complicate the issue.

Coleman v HM Advocate (1999): where a mob becomes murderous, no member of that mob can be convicted of the murder purely on the basis of his membership of the mob. It must also be proved that he shared the mob's murderous purpose.

Sloan v Macmillan (1922): there is no minimum number of members to constitute a mob.

12 CRIMES AGAINST THE COURSE OF JUSTICE

There is some ambiguity in Scots law as to whether there is, in fact, a category of crimes against the course of justice or whether there is only one such crime – attempting to pervert the course of justice – and all offences which would otherwise fall into this category are really just examples of this. A crime like perjury, for instance, is also an attempt to prevent the course of justice from running its proper course. Current practice seems to be that if there is a specific named offence, and the accused satisfies the *actus reus* and *mens rea* for that (for example, perjury), then that is what will be charged. Anything else will be swept up as an attempt to pervert the course of justice. We will therefore look at specific crimes separately.

FALSE REPORTING TO POLICE; WASTING THE TIME OF THE POLICE; MISLEADING THE POLICE; GIVING FALSE INFORMATION TO THE CRIMINAL AUTHORITIES

These are all basically the same crime, though it can be called by any of these names. It can be committed in one of two ways. Hume (i, 341) recognised that it was a crime to make a false accusation that a particular, named individual had committed an offence. The *mens rea* seems to be knowledge that the story was untrue. This is what happened in the modern case of *Simpkins* v *HM Advocate* (1985), where a store detective concocted a shoplifting charge against two boys. The police were informed and they investigated so that the two boys were under suspicion for a period. Simpkins was convicted of falsely accusing two persons in a shop of having committed the crime of theft and of fabricating evidence tending to support that false accusation which was reported to the police.

The other way in which this crime can be committed is simply by giving information to the police (or possibly to the procurator fiscal) which causes them to commence an investigation. Here, the accused does not have to implicate a specific individual – indeed he or she does not even have to allege that a crime has been committed. The first time the charge was used was in the case of *Kerr* v *Hill* (1936), where the accused simply alleged that he had seen a cyclist being knocked down in Paisley, by a bus run by Young's bus company. Lord Justice-General Normand stated that "the giving to the police of information known to be false, for the purpose of causing them to institute an investigation with a view to criminal proceedings, is in itself a crime" (at 75). His view was that "the essence of the crime" consisted in the fact that "the criminal authorities were deliberately set in motion by a malicious person by means of an invented story" (at 75).

This view was carried forward in the case of *Gray* v *Morrison* (1954). Here, the accused had refused a lift home from a friend, stating, falsely, that he planned to cycle home. When the friend discovered that Gray's bicycle was not where he said he had left it, he assumed it had been stolen. Gray felt obliged to report it to the police in case his friend wondered why he had not. Gray was convicted of falsely representing to a police sergeant that a pedal cycle belonging to him had been stolen, and thereby causing officers of the local constabulary to waste their time in the investigation of this false story. In his judgment Lord Justice-General Cooper indicated that the charge should always specify that the accused knew that the information was false. This, therefore, constitutes the *mens rea*. It does not matter whether or not the statement was made maliciously.

PERJURY

Witnesses in judicial proceedings swear an oath or affirmation to tell the truth. If, having taken the oath, they give evidence which is not true, they can be charged with perjury.

A number of points must be established before a charge of perjury can be brought:

(1) The evidence must be given in judicial proceedings. This obviously applies to courts but it would apply equally in proceedings before a tribunal if it was empowered to take evidence on oath.

(2) The statement must be definite and unequivocal. If it is ambiguous, and one interpretation would be true, the accused must receive the benefit of this doubt.

(3) The witness may say that he does not remember the event about which he is being questioned. If it can be proved that he *does* remember, the statement can be prosecuted as perjury. A similar point is illustrated in *Simpson* v *Tudhope* (1988). The accused was a serving police officer who was convicted of perjury on the basis of definite evidence which he gave that he had been accompanied, on a particular occasion, by a female police officer. In fact, he could not recollect whether he had been accompanied by her or by a male colleague. It was a lie, and, hence, perjury, to state that he had

been accompanied by A when the truth was that he did not know whether he had been accompanied by A or by B.

(4) The false statement must be relevant to the point at issue in the case, or to the credibility of the (accused) witness. In *Lord Advocate's Reference (No 1 of 1985)* (1986), the accused had previously been a Crown witness in a murder trial. While he was giving evidence at that trial, on oath, it was put to him that he had made a statement to the police during an earlier interview. He denied making such a statement. On the basis of this denial, he was charged with, but subsequently acquitted of, perjury. The Lord Advocate referred the matter to the High Court on a point of law. It was held that perjury consists simply in making a false statement under oath. Here the perjury was the denial that the accused had ever made such a statement to the police. The truth or falsity of the alleged statement itself, and any issue as to whether it had been lawfully obtained, were irrelevant in a perjury case. Second, the High Court held that any evidence which is competent and relevant either in proof of the charge in the original case or in relation to the witness's credibility can ground a perjury charge.

(5) To satisfy the *mens rea* requirement for perjury, the false evidence must be given wilfully.

SUBORNATION OF PERJURY

This consists in inducing – by any means – threat, bribe or simple persuasion – someone to give perjured evidence. The witness must actually give the perjured evidence in order for the crime to be complete. Where an accused tries to suborn perjury but the witness tells the truth in court or, for some other reason, the perjured evidence is not given, the charge is attempted subornation of perjury.

ATTEMPTING TO PERVERT THE COURSE OF JUSTICE

As already noted, all of the foregoing offences could be prosecuted as an attempt to pervert the course of justice. It is necessary now to consider the circumstances where this is the crime actually charged. This form of charge was first used in 1946 in the case of *Scott* v *HM Advocate* (1946), where the facts were that the accused had tried to persuade two women to give false evidence that, at a time when he had actually been involved in a car accident, he had been in their house. Clearly, this could have been charged as attempted subornation of perjury. In *Dalton* v *HM Advocate* (1951), however, no other nominate crime had been committed. Here, the accused tried to induce a witness not to identify a robbery suspect in a police identity parade. The court held that attempting to pervert the course of justice in this way did constitute a crime.

The word "attempt" here is largely redundant and it is not being used, as in relation to inchoate crimes, in the sense of a criminal attempt. It is equally appropriate to charge exactly the same conduct as "perverting the course of justice" and this is sometimes done.

Actus reus

The *actus reus* is the behaviour which gets in the way of the smooth progress of the course of justice. Words used to describe this in charges include "hinder", "obstruct", "pervert" and "defeat". There must be a course of justice in existence but this exists at a very early stage. In *Watson* v *HM Advocate* (1993), it was held that the course of justice begins at the point when the police begin to investigate an incident before they even know whether that incident constituted a crime.

Mens rea

The *mens rea* for attempting to pervert the course of justice is evil intention. In *HM Advocate* v *Mannion* (1961), Lord Justice-Clerk Thomson stated this clearly as follows: "[e]vil intention, of course, is of the essence of the matter and must be established. This indictment clearly narrates the evil intention of the accused to avoid being called upon to give evidence" (at 80). In this case, the accused deliberately left his home and went into hiding in order to avoid giving evidence in the trial of a third party for aggravated theft. The court held that this did constitute an attempt to pervert the course of justice, even though Mannion had not actually been cited to appear as a witness at that point.

The course of justice continues until a convicted person has completed her sentence. Sometimes, therefore, the course of justice is perverted by something which happens much later in the process, in relation to people who are being held in lawful custody.

PRISON BREAKING

It is clearly an offence – known as prison breaking and recognised by Hume (i, 401) – to escape from prison. It applies only to an escape from a prison itself – not to escape from police cells or any other similar place.

ESCAPING FROM LAWFUL CUSTODY

Sometimes, an individual may escape not from prison itself but from somewhere else where he is lawfully detained. In *HM Advocate* v *Martin* (1956), one of the three co-accused had been taken to form part of a prison working party. He escaped from there with the help of his two co-accused and was convicted of attempting to defeat the ends of justice by absconding from lawful custody. In *McAllister* v *HM Advocate* (1987), the accused escaped from the toilets at Edinburgh Royal Infirmary. He had been escorted there from Saughton Prison by two prison officers so that he could have X-rays carried out. He was convicted of escaping from lawful custody and attempting to defeat the ends of justice.

CONTEMPT OF COURT

Contempt of court is not a crime as such but it can be punished by a fine or by imprisonment, so it bears most of the hallmarks of a criminal offence. It has been described as "a *sui generis* offence committed against the court itself which it is peculiarly within the province of the court to punish" (*Robertson and Gough* v *HM Advocate* (2007) per Lord Justice-Clerk Gill at para 31). The same case offered the following definition:

> "Contempt of court is constituted by conduct that denotes wilful defiance of, or disrespect towards, the court or that wilfully challenges or affronts the authority of the court or the supremacy of the law itself, whether in civil or criminal proceedings" (*Robertson and Gough* v *HM Advocate* (2008) per Lord Justice-Clerk Gill at para 29).

Actus reus

The behavioural element consists in any behaviour which challenges the authority of the court. For example, in *Young* v *Lees* (1998), the accused had previously been removed from Edinburgh Sheriff Court during the trial of his cohabitee because of his behaviour. His partner was remanded in custody, at which point he opened the court door and shouted "You guffy" (at 560) at the sheriff. He was found to be in contempt of court and sentenced to 60 days in prison.

Mens rea

The accused's conduct must be wilful. Contempt of court cannot be committed recklessly. In *McMillan* v *Carmichael* (1994), the accused was held to be in contempt of court because he yawned, noisily and unrestrainedly, while sitting at the back of the court. The accused's explanation that he had not been aware of what he was doing was rejected by the sheriff. On appeal, the High Court held that an intention to challenge or affront the authority of the court was a prerequisite of contempt of court and this was not made out here. The conviction was quashed.

Similarly, in *Caldwell* v *Normand* (1994), the accused turned up half an hour late for his assault case in the district court in Glasgow because he had slept in. The justice found him to be in contempt. This was quashed on appeal because the justice had not made any attempt to establish whether the accused was wilfully defying the order of the court or intending disrespect to the court.

Procedures

Contemptuous behaviour can be directed either against the administration of justice itself, within that court, or against a judge more personally. A good example of the former is where a witness prevaricates in giving evidence. This is a clear example of contempt of court as in the Robertson part of *Robertson and Gough* v *HM Advocate* (2007). Where the contempt is of this type, the presiding judge can deal with it him or herself, applying the procedural safeguards set out in paras 83–100 of the case. Where the contempt is directed against the judge personally, the matter should be referred to another judge or panel of judges as in *Anwar, Respondent* (2008). *Robertson and Gough* states expressly that the procedure followed in *Young* v *Lees* (1998), where the trial judge himself sentenced the contemnor to 60 days in prison, is no longer acceptable (at para 79).

Essential Facts

- All crimes which come into the category of offences against the course of justice could be prosecuted as attempting to pervert the course of justice. The more common practice is, however, to charge an accused with a nominate crime, such as perjury, where his actions satisfy its requirements and only to charge with attempting to pervert the course of justice itself where no other crime is applicable.

- It is a criminal offence either to make a false accusation to the police that a named individual has committed an offence or to give information to the police (or to the procurator fiscal) which causes an investigation to be started. In both cases, the *mens rea* is knowledge that the story is untrue.

- Perjury consists in wilfully (ie intentionally) giving untrue evidence on oath in judicial proceedings, whether before a court or a tribunal. The disputed evidence must be competent and relevant either in the original case in which the perjury accused was a witness or in relation to his credibility generally.

- Subornation of perjury is inducing, by any means, another person to give perjured evidence. The crime is only complete if that evidence is, in fact, given. Otherwise, the accused could be convicted of attempted subornation of perjury.

- The crime of attempting to pervert the course of justice covers a very wide range of behaviour. The *actus reus* is the behaviour which obstructs, at any point in its course, the otherwise smooth flow of the course of justice. The *mens rea* is evil intention so to obstruct.

- The course of justice starts as soon as the police begin to investigate an incident, even before it is clear that a crime has been committed. It continues until any sentence imposed by the court has been served.

- Contempt of court is not, strictly a crime. It can, however, be punished by a fine or by imprisonment so it is generally treated as a form of criminal behaviour. The *actus reus* is any behaviour which challenges the authority of the court. To constitute the *mens rea*, the accused's conduct must be wilful.

- Where the contempt is directed against the administration of justice, the trial judge may deal with it herself. Where it is directed against the judge personally, the matter must be referred to another judge or panel of judges.

Essential Cases

Kerr v Hill (1936): it is a crime to give false information to the police which causes them to commence an investigation.

Gray v Morrison (1954): the *mens rea* of giving false information to the police is knowledge of the falsity of the information. The information does not have to be given maliciously.

Lord Advocate's Reference (No 1 of 1985) (1986): the issue in a perjury trial is simply whether or not the accused lied under oath. Any issue as to whether the evidence in the original trial was lawfully obtained is, therefore, irrelevant. Evidence can ground a perjury charge provided it was relevant to the original trial and/or that it goes to the credibility of the witness (now accused).

Dalton v HM Advocate (1951): behaviour which gets in the way of the smooth running of the course of justice constitutes the crime of attempting to pervert the course of justice.

Watson v HM Advocate (1993): the course of justice begins as soon as the police begin to investigate an incident, whether or not it is clear at that point that a crime has been committed.

HM Advocate v Mannion (1961): the *mens rea* of attempting to pervert the course of justice is evil intention.

McMillan v Carmichael (1994): contempt of court must be committed wilfully or intentionally before it can attract criminal sanctions.

Robertson and Gough v HM Advocate (2007): defines contempt of court and explains the procedural safeguards to ensure it is dealt with fairly when it arises.

13 SEXUAL OFFENCES

INTRODUCTION

This is a transitional period in the area of sexual offences in Scots criminal law. The Sexual Offences (Scotland) Act 2009 was enacted on 14 July of that year but, at the time of writing, had not yet been brought into force. Until that happens, the law governing the area remains the common law (together with pre-existing legislation) and, because the Act will not have retrospective effect, even thereafter, there will be a period when the old law and the new statutory regime will operate alongside each other. Anyone who commits a sexual offence prior to the Act being brought into force will be prosecuted under the old law. Eventually, the common law will cease to have effect in most areas, because the Act abolishes its rules on rape, clandestine injury to women, lewd, indecent or libidinous practices or behaviour and sodomy (s 52(a)). At present, however, it is necessary to consider both the Act and, rather more briefly, the pre-existing provisions.

SEXUAL OFFENCES (SCOTLAND) ACT 2009

Consent

One of the main innovations of the Act is that it introduces a statutory definition of consent which applies to all of the offences which the Act creates where consent is at issue. These are rape (s 1); sexual assault by penetration (s 2); sexual assault (s 3); sexual coercion (s 4); coercing a person into being present during a sexual activity (s 5); coercing a person into looking at a sexual image (s 6); communicating indecently (s 7(1)); causing a person to see or hear an indecent communication (s 7(2)); sexual exposure (s 8); and voyeurism (other than where the offence consists in installing equipment or constructing or adapting a structure to enable other forms of the offence to be carried out) (s 9). To constitute these offences, the proscribed conduct must be carried out both without consent and without any *reasonable* belief on the accused's part that the victim did consent. The requirement that any belief in consent must be held on reasonable grounds, rather than simply being held genuinely, is a welcome improvement on the common law. (It should be noted that administering a substance for a sexual purpose (s 11) is contained within Pt 1 of the

Act, to which the consent provisions apply, but it is based on the victim's *knowledge* rather than his or her consent.) In ascertaining whether any belief in consent (or, where appropriate, knowledge) was reasonable, "regard is to be had to whether the [accused] took any steps to ascertain whether there was consent or ... knowledge; and if so, to what those steps were" (s 16).

Consent – definition

Section 12 defines consent generally, for the purposes of all of the relevant offences listed above, as "free agreement". The Act (s 13(2)) sets down six sets of circumstances in which consent is automatically deemed to be absent. These are:

- where the victim is incapable because of the effect of alcohol or any other substance of consenting to it;
- where the victim agrees or submits to the conduct because of violence used, or threats of violence, against him or her or any other person;
- where the victim agrees or submits to the conduct because he or she is unlawfully detained by the accused;
- where the victim agrees or submits to the conduct because he or she is mistaken, as a result of deception by the accused, as to the nature or purpose of the conduct;
- where the victim agrees or submits to the conduct because the accused induces him or her to agree or submit to the conduct by impersonating a person known personally to him or her; or
- where the only expression or indication of agreement to the conduct is from a person other than the victim.

In any situation apart from these six, the issue of whether or not consent exists will be governed by the general definition ("free agreement") in s 12.

In relation to all of the offences listed above, (other than administering a substance for a sexual purpose) the following points apply:

- the victim may withdraw consent at any time and, where the conduct is continuing conduct such as penetration, consent may be withdrawn *during* the conduct, making any further or continued conduct thereafter non-consensual (s 15(3) and (4)).
- "[a] person is incapable, while asleep or unconscious, of consenting to any conduct" (s 14(2)).
- "a mentally disordered person is incapable of consenting to conduct where, by reason of mental disorder, the person is unable to do one or more of the following –

(a) understand what the conduct is,

(b) form a decision as to whether to engage in the conduct (or as to whether the conduct should take place),

(c) communicate any such decision" (s 17(2)).

Each of the offences created in ss 1–9 and 11 (and listed above) will now be considered. The phrase "without consent" will be used to signify the need both for the absence of the victim's consent *and* the absence of any reasonable belief on the accused's part in such consent.

Rape (s 1)

The *actus reus* of rape is constituted by penetration to any extent, without consent, of the victim's vagina, anus or mouth by the accused's penis. This requirement of penile penetration means that the crime can be committed only by a male person. The victim can be either male or female. "Penis" and "vagina" are both defined specifically to include surgically constructed organs (s 1(4)). "Penetration" is defined as a continuing act (s 1(2) and (3)) so that the victim can retract consent at any time prior to withdrawal of the penis, thereby rendering the act non-consensual and, hence, rape, from that point.

The 2009 Act has not substantially changed the *mens rea* of rape from the common law position (other than in relation to the need for any belief in consent to be reasonable) but the drafting of the statutory provision is perhaps rather opaque. The accused must intend the penetration without any reasonable belief in the victim's consent to this act, or else he must be "reckless as to whether there is penetration" (s 1(1)).

Sexual assault by penetration (s 2)

While s 1 of the Act expands the definition of rape from that existing at common law, it can still only be committed by the accused "with his penis". Section 2 creates a new offence of sexual assault by penetration which consists in penetration, to any extent, without consent, of the vagina or anus (but not the mouth) of the victim by any part of the accused's body (including the penis (s 2(4)) or anything else (s 2(1)). The *mens rea* is identical to that for rape and there is the same provision relating to the withdrawal of consent by the victim *during* the conduct. Both crimes can be prosecuted only on indictment (s 48 and Sch 2). The maximum penalty for both is life imprisonment and a fine – though it is not competent to impose only a fine for either (s 48 and Sch 2). It is therefore difficult to distinguish between them in terms of seriousness.

Sexual assault (s 3)

Where the relevant conduct is carried out without consent, s 3 of the Act specifically proscribes the following:

- sexual penetration, by any means (including by the accused's penis – s 3(5)) and to any extent of the victim's vagina, anus or mouth. The *mens rea* is the same as that for rape;

- sexual touching of the victim. The *mens rea* requires that this is done intentionally or recklessly;

- engagement in any other form of sexual activity in which the accused has physical contact (whether bodily contact or contact by means of an implement and whether or not through clothing) with the victim. The *mens rea* is, again, that this is done intentionally or recklessly;

- the ejaculation of semen by the accused onto the victim. The *mens rea* is that this is done intentionally or recklessly;

- the emission of urine or saliva by the accused onto the victim sexually. The *mens rea* is, once more, that the accused does this intentionally or recklessly.

These behaviours would have come within the ambit of indecent assault at common law, yet the Act does not abolish those rules – presumably because the view was taken that the common law crime constituted a species of assault of which the indecent circumstances were simply an aggravation, rather than a sexual offence in its own right. Nonetheless, this must, at least leave some scope for confusion in the future as to whether to prosecute (common law) indecent assault or the appropriate form of sexual assault from the foregoing statutory list.

Offences involving coercion (ss 4–6)

Sections 4–6 criminalise various forms of coercion in a sexual context. "Sexual coercion" (s 4) arises where the accused causes the victim, without consent, to participate in a sexual activity. The *mens rea* requires that this should be done intentionally. According to s 60, an activity "is sexual if a reasonable person would, in all the circumstances of the case, consider it to be sexual."

Section 5 makes it a criminal offence to coerce the victim into being present during a sexual activity and s 6 to coerce the victim into looking at a sexual image, in both cases, without consent, for the purpose either of obtaining sexual gratification (ss 5(2)(a) and 6(2)(a)) or of humiliating, alarming or distressing the victim (ss 5(2)(b) and 6(2)(b)). In relation to all three offences, the *mens rea* is that these actions should be undertaken intentionally. It is immaterial, in relation to s 5, whether the accused himself engages in the sexual activity or whether he causes the victim to be present while a third party does so (s 5(1)). The sexual activity still takes place in the vcictim's presence if it occurs in a place where the victim can observe it (s 5(3)).

Section 6(3) defines "sexual image" as an image of the accused, a third person or an imaginary person engaging in a sexual activity or of the genitals of one of those people.

Communicating indecently (s 7(1)); Causing a person to see or hear an indecent communication (s 7(2))

In term of s 7(1), it is an offence for the accused to send a "sexual written communication" or direct a "sexual verbal communication", by whatever means, to the victim, without consent, for the purpose of obtaining sexual gratification or of humiliating, alarming or distressing the victim. Section 7(2) criminalises, in identical terms to s 7(1) as to consent and purpose, causing the victim to see a sexual written communication or to hear a sexual verbal communication.The *mens rea* of each of these offences is that the relevant activity should be carried out intentionally.

"Written communication" means a communication in "whatever written form" including something not written by the accused such as "a passage in a book or magazine" (s 7(4)(a)). "Verbal communication" mean a communication "in whatever verbal form" and includes sounds of actual or simulated sexual activity and sign language (s 7(4)(b)).

In terms of s 60, a communication is sexual if "a reasonable person would, in all the circumstances of the case, consider it to be sexual."

Sexual exposure (s 8)

Exposure, by the accused, without consent, of the accused's genitals to the victim, in a sexual manner, with the intention that the victim will see them, for the purpose of either sexual gratification or humiliating, alarming or distressing the victim, constitutes the crime of sexual exposure. The *mens rea* is that this should be done intentionally. In *Webster* v *Dominick* (2003) Lord Justice-Clerk Gill stated that indecent exposure was the "paradigm case" (para 53) of the common law crime of public indecency (discussed below). The Act does not specifically abolish this crime. As with sexual assault then, there may be scope for confusion as to which offence to prosecute where this conduct occurs, once the Act is in force.

Voyeurism (s 9)

The Act specifies four separate forms of the crime of voyeurism. The first three forms, but not the fourth, must be carried out without consent and must be done either for the purpose of the sexual gratification of the accused or (in relation to the second and third forms only) either the accused or another person or (in all three cases) for the purpose of humiliating, distressing or alarming the victim. The four forms are:

- the accused observing the victim doing a private act;
- the accused operating equipment with the intention of enabling himself or another person to observe the victim doing a private act;
- the accused recording the victim doing a private act with the intention that the accused or another person will look at the image of the victim doing the act;
- the accused installing equipment or constructing or adapting a structure, or part thereof, with the intention of enabling the accused or another person to carry out one of the three preceding forms of the offence.

"For the purposes of [all forms of the voyeurism offence], a person is doing a private act if the person is in a place which in the circumstances would reasonably be expected to provide privacy, and –

(a) the person's genitals, buttocks or breasts are exposed or covered only with underwear,

(b) the person is using a lavatory, or

(c) the person is doing a sexual act that is not of a kind ordinarily done in public" (s 10).

Administering a substance for sexual purposes (s 11)

This offence arises where the accused intentionally administers a substance to the victim, or causes the victim to take a substance, without the victim's knowledge and with no reasonable belief that the victim knows, for the purpose of stupefying or overpowering the victim so as to enable any person to engage in a sexual activity which involves the victim.

"For the purposes of [this offence], if [the accused], whether by act or omission, induces in [the victim] a reasonably belief that the substance administered or taken is (either or both) –

(a) of a substantially lesser strength, or

(b) in a substantially lesser quantity,

than it is, any knowledge [or belief as to knowledge] which [the victim] has that it is being administered or taken is to be disregarded" (s 11(2)).

In other words, if the accused, for the purpose of enabling any person to engage in a sexual activity which involves the victim, leads the victim reasonably to believe that he is ingesting substantially less of the intoxicating substance than is, in fact, the case, then this constitutes an offence in its own right.

OFFENCES AGAINST CHILDREN

The Act creates specific versions of each of the offences listed above (other than administering a substance for sexual purposes) which apply only where the victim is a child. Sections 18–26 apply to a "young child" (aged 12 or under) and ss 28–36 to an "older child" (aged 13, 14 or 15). None of these offences makes any provision concerning the victim's consent, presumably because children are, for these purposes, deemed incapable of giving consent. Thus, "rape of a young child" (s 18), for example, is constituted simply by intentional or reckless penetration, by the accused with his penis, of the vagina, anus or mouth of the victim. "Causing an older child to participate in a sexual activity" (s 31) requires only that the accused intentionally caused a child of the requisite age so to participate. The offences which relate to older children (ss 28–36) all require that the accused should be aged 16 or over. There is no offence of "rape of an older child". Instead, the relevant crime is named "having intercourse with an older child" (s 28).

It is an offence for older children to engage in sexual conduct with each other (s 37). The proscribed behaviours are sexual penetration by the accused, with his penis, and to any extent, either intending to do so or reckless as to whether there is penetration, of the victim's vagina, anus or mouth (s 37(3)(a)) or intentionally or recklessly touching the victim's vagina, anus or penis sexually with the accused's mouth (s 37(3)(b)). If the "victim" consents to the conduct, then she or he also commits an offence (s 37(4)). "Consent" is specially defined for the purposes of s 37 by s 38 but the definition is the same as the general definition outlined above (see section of this chapter headed "Consent").

Defences to offences against children

It is no defence to any offence committed against a young child (ss 18–26) that the accused believed that the victim had attained 13 years of age (s 27).

With regard to older children, it is generally a defence that the accused reasonably believed that the victim had attained the age of 16 (s 39(1)) but this defence is not available if the accused has previously been charged by the police with a relevant sexual offence (all of which are sexual offences committed against children or young people) or if she or he is the subject of a risk of sexual harm order (s 39(2)). (Such an order would be issued by a court, in certain circumstances, where the chief constable of any area had reason to believe that an individual had engaged a child on at least two occasions in certain sexual activities or matters.)

It is also a defence to some of the sexual offences against an older child that, at the time of the conduct, the difference between the ages of the accused and the victim did not exceed 2 years (s 39(3)). The defence is *in*applicable to offences which involve either penile penetration or sexual touching by the accused's mouth. It is also inapplicable to intentionally or recklessly emitting urine or saliva onto the victim.

ABUSE OF POSITIONS OF TRUST

Part 5 of the Act criminalises sexual behaviour by adults towards children with whom they are in a position of trust and by carers towards the mentally disordered where a similar relationship exists.

Sexual abuse of trust: children

Section 42 creates the offence of sexual abuse of trust. It is committed where the accused, who must be aged 18 or over, intentionally engages in a sexual activity with, or directed towards, the victim who is aged under 18 and the accused is in a position of trust towards the victim. People in positions of trust include those who look after the child in a residential or hospital setting, teachers and parents (s 43).

Defences (s 45)

The following are defences to the crime of sexual abuse of trust:

- that the accused reasonably believed that the victim was aged 18 or over or that the accused was not in a position of trust towards the child-victim;
- that the victim is the accused's spouse or civil partner;
- that immediately before the position of trust came into existence, a sexual relationship existed between the accused and the victim.

Sexual abuse of trust: mentally disordered persons (s 46)

The offence of sexual abuse of trust of a mentally disordered person is committed where the accused intentionally engages in a sexual activity with, or directed towards, the victim (who is a mentally disordered person) where the accused is either providing care services to the victim or else works for a hospital, independent health care service or state hospital which is treating the victim.

Defences (s 47)

The defences to sexual abuse of trust of a mentally disordered person are:

- that the accused reasonably believed that the victim was not mentally disordered;
- that the accused reasonably believed that he was not in the position of trust as defined by s 46;
- that the victim was the accused's civil partner or spouse;
- in certain circumstances, that the accused and the victim had been in a sexual relationship immediately before they came into the position of trust.

COMMON LAW (AND PRE-EXISTING LEGISLATION) ON SEXUAL OFFENCES

This part of the chapter will outline the "old" law on sexual offences, that is to say, the law which pre-existed the 2009 Act, which remains current until the Act is brought into force and which will continue to be of some relevance thereafter (see the introduction to this chapter). It also discusses those areas of the law which are unchanged by the Act.

Incest

The law on incest is not changed by the Sexual Offences (Scotland) Act 2009. It is still based on the book of Leviticus in the Bible though this has been translated into a statutory table indicating the forbidden degrees of relationship, between which sexual intercourse is prohibited. This table is set down in s 1 of the Criminal Law (Consolidation) (Scotland) Act 1995.

The forbidden degrees are: parent and child; grandparent and grandchild; brother and sister; aunt (uncle) and nephew (niece); and great grandparent and great grandchild. In addition, adoptive or former adoptive parents are prohibited from having sexual intercourse with their adoptive or former adoptive children. Illegitimacy is irrelevant and half-blood relationships are also covered.

Section 1 also provides a number of defences to a charge of incest: (1) that the person did not know and had no reason to suspect that the other person was within the forbidden degrees (s 1(1)(a)); (2) that the person did not consent to the intercourse (s 1(1)(b)); and (3) that the person was married to the other at the time by a marriage entered into outside Scotland and recognised as valid by Scots law (s 1(1)(c)). The onus of proof is on the accused on the balance of probabilities.

Incest consists in heterosexual penetrative intercourse but both male and female participants commit the crime.

Common law rape

"[T]he general rule is that the actus reus of rape is constituted by the man having sexual intercourse with the woman without her consent" (*Lord Advocate's Reference (No 1 of 2001)* (2002) per Lord Justice-General Cullen, at p 476). Thus, the victim must be female. Non-consensual anal intercourse committed against one man by another, is not common law rape and would probably be prosecuted as indecent assault.

Rape is constituted by penetration of the vagina by the penis. No other form of penetration suffices. The degree of penetration is unimportant – it may be very minor – and there is no need for emission of semen. If the intercourse is non-consensual then it can be prosecuted as rape no matter the age of the victim.

Only a male person can be charged with common law rape. It is theoretically possible for a woman to be guilty of rape on an art and part basis.

Lord Advocate's Reference (No 1 of 2001) (2002) reviewed the law of rape in its historical context, determining that an earlier decision which appeared to insist on the use of force (*Charles Sweenie* (1858)) – so that the rape was carried out "against the victim's will" – had been wrongly decided. Instead, the absence of consent on the part of the complainer is the crucial matter. Thus, the Crown must prove, beyond reasonable doubt, that the intercourse took place without her consent. This constitutes part of the *actus reus*. The *mens rea* is concerned only with the *accused's* attitude towards the criminal act.

It is accepted both at common law (*C v HM Advocate* (1987)) and by statute (Criminal Law (Consolidation) (Scotland) Act 1995, s 5(1)) that girls aged 12 and under are incapable of consenting, therefore intercourse with them is rape (or "unlawful sexual intercourse" in terms of the 1995

Act). The statutory protection extends to girls aged under 16 (s 5(3)). Where the girl is aged 13, 14 or 15, it is a defence either that the accused had reasonable cause to believe that she was his wife or that he is aged under 24, has not previously been charged with a similar offence and has reasonable cause to believe that she is aged 16 or over (s 5(5)). These provisions of the 1995 Act will be expressly repealed by the 2009 Act (Sch 6) when it is brought into force.

The common law recognises that a woman may also be incapable of consenting due to mental disorder. If consent is not given, the accused can be charged with rape but this also constitutes a statutory offence under the Mental Health (Care and Treatment) (Scotland) Act 2003, s 311. The victim here could be either male or female and the section criminalises vaginal or anal intercourse and any other sexual act. It is a defence that the accused did not know, and could not reasonably have been expected to know, that the victim suffered from a mental disorder and that she was incapable of consenting (s 311(5)). This s 311 will also be repealed when the 2009 Act comes into force.

Two other issues require some discussion:

(a) Intercourse obtained by impersonation:

In *William Fraser* (1847), the accused obtained sexual intercourse with a woman by pretending to be her husband, an act which was held to be a form of fraud rather than rape. The view of the court was that this did not constitute rape because the victim consented to the intercourse itself – just not with that person.

The principle that this does not constitute rape was applied in *Gray v Criminal Injuries Compensation Board* (1999). June Gray's husband was a bigamist. This meant that her marriage to him was a sham. She argued that her consent to sex with him was predicated on being married to him. It was held that he had committed fraud, rather than rape.

On the other hand, in *Allan v HM Advocate* (2004), the victim had sexual intercourse with the accused because she thought that he was her boyfriend. This appears to have been treated as a straightforward case of rape. There is no reference to *Fraser*, possibly because the accused made no attempt to deceive her, so that he could not have been charged with fraud.

It is a statutory offence to have intercourse with a woman by impersonating her husband in terms of the Criminal Law (Consolidation) (Scotland) Act 1995, s 7(3). This provision relates only to parties who are actually married. Again, this subsection will be specifically repealed when the 2009 Act comes into force.

(b) Clandestine injury to women: as already noted, the decision
in *Charles Sweenie* (1858) was directly overruled by the *Lord Advocate's
Reference (No 1 of 2001)* (2002). Nonetheless, certain of the issues which it
raises remain relevant in the common law. Charles Sweenie had intercourse
with a woman who was asleep throughout the proceedings. The court
declined to call this rape because the victim's will had not been overcome.
Behaviour of this nature became known as the crime of clandestine injury
to women.

Following the *Lord Advocate's Reference (No 1 of 2001)* (2002), the
position is that, if a woman is unable to give her consent for any reason
– including because she is naturally asleep, or because she is under the
influence of alcohol or drugs – it is rape to have sexual intercourse with
her. Lord Cullen stated that the woman requires to give *active* consent
(at 475). Her inability to express an opinion one way or the other due
to her consumption of alcohol, or to any other cause, means that she
is not actively consenting and any intercourse with her will amount to
rape.

The current definition of rape at common law obviated the need for the
crime of clandestine injury to women but the matter will be put beyond
doubt when the 2009 Act comes into force. It specifically abolishes that
crime (s 52(a)(ii)).

Common law rape: mens rea

At common law, according to Lord Justice-Clerk Gill in *McKearney* v *HM
Advocate* (2004), "the *mens rea* of [rape] consists of an intention on the part
of the accused to have intercourse with the complainer, together with
knowledge on his part that she does not consent, or with recklessness on
his part as whether or not she does" (at 90).

The *mens rea* of recklessness arises if the accused was completely
indifferent as to whether or not the sex was consensual – if he was going
to have intercourse with the victim no matter what – even though he
actually had no idea whether she consented. With regard to intention,
if the accused *thought* that the victim consented, and he can prove this,
then, even if she did not, in fact, consent, he will be acquitted. This
belief in the victim's consent only has to be held honestly. Following
on the cases of *Meek* v *HM Advocate* (1982) and *Jamieson* v *HM Advocate*
(1994), there is no need for the belief to be reasonable. Nonetheless, if
the accused's grounds for assuming consent are obviously spurious, the
chances of the jury believing that he truly thought the victim consented
are diminished.

Following *McKearney*, there has been a tendency to divide rape appeals into two categories. Where it is proved that force was used to achieve penetration, (as, for example, in *Gordon* v *HM Advocate* (2004)) this sets up a presumption that the victim did not consent and that the accused knew this: he would not have had to use violence if she was consenting. In any case where there is no evidence of force, and the issue turns on the presence or absence of the victim's consent, and the accused's state of mind in relation to this, the jury must be specifically instructed on the honest belief point. The Crown must also lead corroborated evidence to establish either the accused's knowledge of the victim's lack of consent or his recklessness.

Indecent assault

Because of the restricted definition of rape in Scots (common) law, indecent assault is currently charged in a wide range of circumstances. Penetration of the victim's vagina with an implement, for example, could not be rape but could be indecent assault at common law.

There are two alternative views on the nature of the crime of indecent assault. The first is that there is only one crime of assault but that its commission in circumstances of indecency is an aggravation of the basic crime. The other view is that indecent assault is a crime in its own right.

The absence of the victim's consent is of the essence of indecent assault. Touching someone sexually with their consent is (usually) not a crime at all. As soon as the accused's actions go beyond what has been consented to, indecent assault can be charged, as in *Young* v *McGlennan* (1991). In that case, the accused was a serving police officer who had been taking part in a light-hearted exchange with the staff of a Kilmarnock hotel in relation to empire biscuits and how these resembled one member of the hotel staff sunbathing. This was, apparently a reference to her being flat-chested. The accused had placed his hand on one of her breasts and said "I don't think so".

He was convicted of assault, and this was upheld on appeal on the basis that the complainer had not consented to the touch and the appellant had no reason to think that she had. The view taken was that he had touched her deliberately for his own sexual gratification. This satisfied the *mens rea*.

As with rape, if the accused genuinely believes that the victim consents to the sexual touching, he must be acquitted. There is no requirement that he should hold this belief on reasonable grounds.

Lewd, indecent and libidinous practices

This has always existed as a crime in Scots law. Its purpose is to protect children from indecency being used against them. The essence of the crime is the tendency to corrupt the innocence of the victim. In order to constitute the crime, indecent practices must be used against a specific victim who is within the class of persons whom the law protects.

Indecent practices

In *Webster* v *Dominick* (2003), Lord Justice-Clerk Gill listed certain practices which, in his view, would constitute the crime. Perhaps the most obvious is indecent physical contact with the victim as in *HM Advocate* v *Millbank* (2002) where the accused had forced two young girls to masturbate him. He was convicted of a separate offence of using lewd, indecent and libidinous practices for taking indecent photographs of approximately 30 other young girls.

In *Dominick*, Lord Gill also specifically included, as an example of an indecent practice, showing indecent videos or photographs to the victim. (The latter practice was the substance of the charge in the case itself.) Finally, he expressed the view that conducting a lewd conversation with the victim, "whether face to face or by a telephone call or through an Internet chat-room" (at para 49), would be sufficient.

Class of victims

The crime of lewd, indecent and libidinous practices protects children aged under, or at, or about, puberty. This is taken to occur at the age of 12 for a girl and at 14 for a boy. *Batty* v *HM Advocate* (1995) may provide limited authority for the view that the class of victims is not limited to those aged at or under, puberty.

It is a statutory offence to use such practices towards any girl aged 12 or over and under 16, in terms of s 6 of the Criminal Law (Consolidation) (Scotland) Act 1995. A similar protection is provided, against homosexual practices, to boys aged under 16 by s 13(5)(c).

It is equally appropriate to charge lewd, indecent and libidinous practices where the victim is male as where she is female.

Mens rea

It appears that the conduct has to be deliberate.

All of this law in relation to children and sexual practices will be abolished when the 2009 Act comes into force.

Public indecency

Where the accused's conduct "affronts public sensibility" (*Webster* v *Dominick* (2003) per Lord Justice-Clerk Gill, at para 50) it may constitute the crime of public indecency.

According to Lord Justice-Clerk Gill's judgment in *Webster* v *Dominick* (2003), the *actus reus* of public indecency has two elements: (1) an indecent act and (2) the effect this has on the minds of the public (at para 53).

(1) The indecent act

The "paradigm case" (para 53) is indecent exposure but other indecent acts also suffice. Lord Gill suggests sexual intercourse in public view or the making of indecent acts or gestures in a stage show. He refuses to commit himself as to whether public indecency extends to acts which are not of a sexual nature, until such cases actually came before the court (para 54).

There is no necessity for the act to take place in a public place. If it is carried out in front of unwilling witnesses, or if it occurred on private premises but was visible to the public, that would be sufficient (para 55). Thus, in *Usai* v *Russell* (2000), the accused had stood naked inside his own house at a window, with the lights on and the curtains fully drawn back, and had been seen touching his genitals. Lord Gill uses this as an example of public indecency committed on private property (at para 55).

(2) The effect on the minds of the public

Lord Gill views public indecency as a public order offence. Whether a particular act is indecent requires to be decided by reference to the circumstances of the case and by changing social standards. He makes reference to the test used by the Canadian courts – the "community standard of tolerance" and the Australian test of "recognised contemporary standards of common propriety." (para 58). The act would need to affront public sensibility.

Public indecency is *not* abolished by the 2009 Act.

Homosexual offences

At common law (consensual) sodomy was a crime constituted by penetration of the anus of one man by the penis of another. Both parties were guilty of the offence. It was legalised in 1980 and the current law is found in the Criminal Law (Consolidation) (Scotland) Act 1995, s 13(1) (where the parties are aged 16 or over and the act is consensual and carried out in private). It is an offence to commit a homosexual act with a person aged under 16 whether or not they are consenting (s 13(5)(c)), unless the accused is aged under 24, has not previously been charged with a like offences and has reasonable cause to believe that the other party was over 16 (s 13(8)).

The 2009 Act applies to both genders in such a way that specific provisions on homosexuality are unnecessary. For the avoidance of doubt, all of this law will be specifically repealed when the Act comes into force.

Essential Facts

(1) Sexual Offences (Scotland) Act 2009

- The Sexual Offences (Scotland) Act 2009, which sweeps away most of the pre-existing law on sexual offences, has been enacted but, at the time of writing, had not yet been brought into force.

- The Act creates new offences of rape; sexual assault by penetration; sexual assault; sexual coercion; coercing a person into being present during a sexual activity; coercing a person into looking at a sexual image; communicating indecently; causing a person to see or hear an indecent communication; sexual exposure; voyeurism and administering a substance for a sexual purpose.

- The Act defines consent as "free agreement" (s 12) for the purposes of each of these offences except the last one. It also specifies six sets of circumstances in which consent is deemed not to be present (s 13(2)).

- Where an accused seeks to rely on the victim's consent as a defence, his belief in that consent must be reasonable.

- The Act creates specific forms of each of its offences where the victim is a young child (aged 12 or under) (ss 18–26) and separate such offences where the victim is an older child (aged 13, 14 or 15) (ss 28–36). Consent is irrelevant to these offences. It is a defence to most sexual offences committed against an older child that the accused reasonably believed the victim to be aged 16 or over but not if the accused has previously been charged with particular sexual offences against children or is the subject of a risk of sexual harm order. It is also a defence to many of the offences against older children that there is no more than a two-year age gap between the accused and the victim

- It is an offence for older children to have sexual intercourse with each other, regardless of consent (s 37).
- The Act also creates offences of sexual abuse of trust to protect children and the mentally disordered from abuse by carers (ss 42–47). It is a defence to most (though not all) such charges that the accused reasonably believed that the victim was aged over 18, or was not mentally disordered respectively; that the accused and the victim were spouses or civil partners; or that they were already in a sexual relationship at the point when they came into the position of trust.

(2) Common law and pre-existing statutory offences

- The *actus reus* of rape consists in a man having sexual intercourse with a woman without her consent. There must be (at least minimal) penetration of the vagina by the penis. To avoid a rape charge, the woman must give active consent. If she is asleep, unconscious or overcome by alcohol or drugs, she cannot consent therefore sexual intercourse with her will, assuming the accused has the appropriate *mens rea*, constitute rape
- Sexual intercourse with girls aged under 16 or with mentally-disordered persons (male or female) who are unable to consent, is prohibited by statute
- The *mens rea* of rape is intention on the part of the accused to have intercourse with the complainer together with knowledge on his part that she does not consent, or with recklessness on his part as to whether or not she does. If the accused honestly believes that she consents then he must be acquitted as he does not have the *mens rea*. He does not have to hold this belief on reasonable grounds
- The *actus reus* of indecent assault is sexual touching without the victim's consent. The *mens rea* is evil intent.
- Lewd, indecent and libidinous practices consists in the use of indecent practices against a girl aged 12 or under or a boy aged 14 or under. Similar statutory offences exist to protect both boys and girls up to the age of 16. The *mens rea* requires that the conduct should be deliberate.
- Public indecency is an indecent act which affronts public sensibility. It must be sufficiently extreme as to go beyond the existing moral consensus on acceptable behaviour. It does not have to be committed in public, provided it has a public dimension.

- (Consensual) sodomy was a crime at common law. This is no longer the case, however, assuming that both parties consent and are aged 16 or over and the act takes place in private.
- Incest consists in heterosexual sexual intercourse between persons who are related to each other in any of the forbidden degrees. These are: parent and child; grandparent and grandchild; brother and sister; aunt (uncle) and nephew (niece); and great grandparent and great grandchild. Both parties commit the crime.

Essential Cases – (Common Law)

Lord Advocate's Reference (No 1 of 2001) (2002): changed the definition of the *actus reus* of rape from sexual intercourse "against the victim's will" to "without her consent".

William Fraser (1847): it is not rape but fraud where the accused obtains sexual intercourse by impersonating the victim's husband because there is still consent, just not to intercourse with that person.

Allan v HM Advocate (2004): the victim had sex with the accused thinking that he was her boyfriend. This constituted rape.

Meek v HM Advocate (1982) and Jamieson v HM Advocate (1994): if the accused is in error as to whether the victim consents, he need only establish that he genuinely believed that she was consenting in order to be acquitted of rape. There is no need for this belief to be held on reasonable grounds.

McKearney v HM Advocate (2004): where the accused does not use force in a rape case, the Crown must lead corroborated evidence on his *mens rea* and the jury must be specifically instructed on the issue of honest belief in consent.

Young v McGlennan (1991): indecent assault consists in sexual touching without the victim's consent. It must be deliberate and for the accused's sexual gratification.

Webster v Dominick (2003): set down the circumstances in which lewd, indecent and libidinous practices and public indecency should each be charged.

14 STATUTORY OFFENCES

Both the Scottish Parliament and, in matters reserved to it under Sch 5 to the Scotland Act 1998 (eg firearms), the United Kingdom Parliament, enact statutory offences which form part of Scots criminal law. Every element of the *actus reus* and the *mens rea* of a statutory offence will be specified in the statute itself. The basic principle is that the courts should give the words used their ordinary meaning. The exact import of a statutory offence is often only apparent after it has been interpreted, sometimes on a number of occasions, by a court.

Sections 47 and 49 of the Criminal Law (Consolidation) (Scotland) Act 1995 respectively prohibit the carrying of offensive weapons and set down an offence of having in a public place an article with a blade or a point. These are good examples of statutory offences.

Section 47(1) states: "[a]ny person who without lawful authority or reasonable excuse, the proof whereof shall lie on him, has with him in any public place any offensive weapon shall be guilty of an offence". Section 49 says: "any person who has an article to which this section applies with him in a public place shall be guilty of an offence [s 49(1)] ... [T]his section applies to any article which has a blade or is sharply pointed [s 49(2)] ...This section does not apply to a folding pocketknife if the cutting edge of its blade does not exceed three inches (7.62 cm) [s 49(3)]. It shall be a defence for a person charged with an offence under subsection (1) above to prove that he had good reason or lawful authority for having the article with him in the public place [s 49(4)]. Without prejudice to the generality of subsection (4) above, it shall be a defence for a person charged with an offence under subsection (1) above to prove that he had the article with him –

(a) for use at work;
(b) for religious reasons; or
(c) as part of any national costume [s 49(5)]."

Under both sections, the basic offence is committed by the accused having the relevant article with him or her in a public place. It must therefore be established that the article meets the terms of the relevant definition (of "offensive weapon", given in s 47(4), or of "article with a blade or which is sharply pointed" as set out above (s 49(2) and (3)), and that the accused was in a public place with it. This illustrates the way in which every essential element of the offence is set out in the statute.

No *mens rea* requirement is apparent on the face of the sections, therefore these may be offences of strict liability (examined below). Defences are provided to each offence. It is a defence to the charge of carrying an offensive weapon that the accused had lawful authority or reasonable excuse for having it with him or her. In relation to having an article with a blade or point, s 49(4) and (5) offer the defences of "good reason", "lawful authority", "for use at work", "for religious reasons" or "as part of any national costume". In all cases, as with many, though not all statutory offences, the onus of proving such a defence shifts to the accused but only on the balance of probabilities. Clearly, it is impossible to know, for example, what will be accepted as a "good reason" until the courts have had the opportunity to interpret that term. Where an accused had just purchased a machete and was taking it home in the wrappings provided by the shop, this was held to constitute a "good reason" (*McGuire* v *Higson* (2003)). On the other hand, in *Crowe* v *Waugh* (1999), the accused's explanation, that he was a keen fisherman who had simply forgotten to take the knife out of his pocket following a fishing expedition 2 days previously, was not. Each case must therefore turn on its own facts.

STRICT LIABILITY

Where a statute specifies *mens rea* for an offence, no question of strict liability arises. Where the statute does not include clear words importing *mens rea*, however, there is always the possibility of strict liability. (*Mens rea* is an essential element of all *common law* crimes.) Strict liability means that the offence has no mental element. If the Crown proves that the accused committed the *actus reus* then, in the absence of any defence, the accused will be convicted. It is usually held to be established only where the statutory provision creating the offence in question cannot otherwise be interpreted so as to make sense. Strict liability raises issues of fairness to the accused since, at the extreme, it could make it possible for her to be convicted of a crime which she was not even aware that she had committed.

The Crown must establish, to the court's satisfaction, as an intrinsic part of the prosecution case, that the offence is one of strict liability.

It is necessary to consider the mechanisms used by the courts to determine whether strict liability applies. In English law, there is a presumption in favour of *mens rea*. In *H* v *Griffiths* (2009) the High Court stated that this was a constitutional principle applicable to Scotland as well. Thus, the Scottish courts also require very good reasons to hold that that presumption does not apply. This is clear from Lord Justice-Clerk Cooper's judgment in *Duguid* v *Fraser* (1942) where he said:

> "[i]n all ... cases [of alleged strict liability] it has, I think, been the practice to insist that the Crown should show that the language, scope and intendment of the statute require that an exception should be admitted to the normal and salutary rule of our law that *mens rea* is an indispensable ingredient of a criminal or quasi-criminal act; and I venture to think that it would be a misfortune if the stringency of this requirement were relaxed" (at 5).

The courts therefore start out from the view that strict liability will not apply and require to be convinced, by the Crown, that it does. Certain principles are applied in making this determination.

Where the offence is "truly criminal" the likelihood is that there will be a *mens rea* requirement. This principle relates to the distinction sometimes drawn in criminal law between things which are wrong in themselves (such as murder or rape), known as *mala in se*, and things which are only wrong because there is a statute prohibiting them, known as *mala prohibita* (such as driving without insurance).

Where the offence is *not* "truly criminal", it is more likely to be classified as strict liability. This is illustrated in the case of *Duguid* v *Fraser* (1942). The case concerned the Prices of Goods Act 1939, a piece of wartime legislation passed to prevent profiteering on certain items which were in short supply. An item covered by the Act was sold for 7s, the price cap being 4s 9d. It was held that strict liability applied. Selling for the highest price available was criminal because the statute declared it to be so – not because it was obviously and morally wrong in itself.

The courts will also consider whether the statute regulates an issue of social concern. If so, this increases the likelihood that strict liability will apply. In *Duguid* v *Fraser* (1942), the statute served the social purpose of preventing profiteering in wartime. In *Crowe* v *Waugh* (1999), the purpose of preventing people carrying knives was an important consideration in the court's determination that the relevant offence was one of strict liability. More generally, the English courts have been particularly proactive in convicting without *mens rea* in relation to pollution. In *Alphacell Ltd* v *Woodward* (1972), a company was convicted of "causing polluting matter to enter the river" despite the fact that it had not been negligent and had taken a number of precautions to prevent pollution.

If holding that strict liability applied would have no effect whatsoever in terms of encouraging adherence, either by the accused or by others, to the terms of the statute, then the existence of *mens rea* is likely to be found. In *Lim Chin Aik* (1963) the accused was charged with remaining in Singapore illegally, after an order had been made prohibiting him from entering the colony. The order identified Lim Chin Aik by name. Nothing whatsoever had, however, been done by the authorities to bring its existence to his attention. On appeal against conviction (which was successful), the Privy Council held that finding Lim Chin Aik guilty would do nothing to encourage anyone else to adhere to the law. Accordingly, strict liability did not apply.

Particular words in statutes

The basic principle is that *mens rea* will only be disapplied by express wording or necessary implication in the statute. It is relatively unusual (though not unheard of – see, for example the Christmas Day and New Year's Day Trading (Scotland) Act 2007, s 6) for a statute actually to state that an offence has no mental element. The door is left open for consideration of strict liability, where the statute does not expressly set down the mental element. Certain words which do not automatically correspond to a mental element have, however, sometimes been interpreted so as to import one.

"Possession"

Possession has been interpreted to require the *mens rea* of knowledge. In *Henvey* v *HM Advocate* (2005) it was accepted that possession (in relation to the supply of illegal drugs) required knowledge of the existence of the relevant item, if not detailed knowledge of its qualities.

"Permitting"

The courts have also interpreted the word "permitting" as requiring knowledge on the part of the accused. In *Mackay Brothers* v *Gibb* (1969), the accused was a garage business which had hired out a car to a man named Sneddon. He had an accident in it and it was found that one of the car's tyres did not have the legally required depth of tread. The firm's garage controller had not specifically checked this before hiring it out. It was held that the controller had "permitted" the car to be used with a defective tyre in breach of the legislation. His "knowledge" was imputed by his failure to check the tyre. He should have done this and, because he had not, he had wilfully blinded himself to the potentially dangerous state of the car.

Similarly, in *Anderson* v *Higson* (2001) the charge was a contravention of s 49(1) of the Civic Government (Scotland) Act 1982 which makes it an offence if any person "suffers or permits any creature in his charge to cause danger or injury to any other person". The court accepted that the phrase "suffers or permits" requires knowledge on the part of the person that the creature is likely to cause alarm or annoyance to others if loose in a public place.

"Causing"

The courts have tended to take a harsher line with the word "causing" – perhaps because its plain meaning is more indicative of action than thought. The case of *Mitchell* v *Morrison* (1938) held that failing to "keep or cause to be kept" a correct record of the hours during which a lorry driver was driving was not an offence which required *mens rea*.

Two English cases concerning the pollution of rivers also illustrate this approach. In *Attorney-General's Reference (No 1 of 1994)* (1995), the court held that the term "causing", in relation to the offence of "causing polluting matter to enter controlled waters" (a river), required some active participation on the part of the accused company but not necessarily its knowledge that the pollution had taken place.

Again, in *Environment Agency* v *Empress Car Co (Abertillery) Ltd* (1999), it was held that Empress did "cause" pollution when an unknown third party opened the unlockable tap on its diesel tank, causing the diesel to drain into a river. This was the case even though Empress did not know until subsequently that this had occurred.

DEFENCES TO STATUTORY OFFENCES

Many statutes (though by no means all) which create strict liability offences also include, alongside these, defences. If a statutory defence is made out, the accused will be acquitted. Where a statute states that the accused must prove a defence, the onus of proof shifts, from the Crown, to the defence. The standard of proof is, however, only on the balance of probabilities. Where it creates a defence but does not specifically require the accused to prove it, the onus of proof remains on the Crown. It must, effectively, disprove, beyond reasonable doubt, the existence of the defence.

"Due diligence" defence

One of the most common statutory defences is that of "due diligence" – that the accused took every possible step to prevent the commission of an offence. An example of this is found in s 6 of the Christmas Day and New Year's Day Trading (Scotland) Act 2007. Sections 1 and 4 of the Act make it an offence for any large shop to open on Christmas Day for the purpose of making retail sales. Section 6 states that it is a defence if the accused proves that they took all reasonable precautions and exercised all due diligence to avoid committing the offence. The Scottish Parliament's Explanatory Note to the Act states that "Th[e] defence is that [the accused] ... had taken all reasonable precautions and had tried to the best of their ability to avoid committing the offence. It is considered that this will require the taking of positive measures such as training staff in their responsibilities."

Overall, to satisfy the due diligence defence, an accused company or individual must establish that they have proper procedures in place to prevent the commission of the relevant offence and that they have taken the appropriate action in relation to the matter actually before the court.

Essential Facts

- All elements of the *actus reus* and, where applicable, the *mens rea* of a statutory offence are to be found in the statute itself.
- Strict liability arises where there is no *mens rea* requirement. All common law crimes require *mens rea*.
- It is for the Crown to establish that any offence is one of strict liability.
- It is a constitutional principle that there is a presumption in favour of *mens rea*.
- The courts are most likely to determine that strict liability exists, where: (1) the offence is wrong in itself (*mala in se*), or "truly criminal", rather than *mala prohibita* or only wrong because a statute declares it to be so; (2) the statute regulates an issue of social concern; (3) the imposition of strict liability is likely to promote greater vigilance in ensuring that the statutory provisions are adhered to.
- The words "possession" and "permit" in statutes have usually been interpreted to require some knowledge on the part of the accused.
- The word "causing" has sometimes been interpreted to import strict liability.

- Some, though by no means all, statutory defences shift the onus of proof onto the accused on the balance of probabilities. A common defence is "due diligence" which requires that the accused has taken all steps to prevent commission of the offence.

Essential Cases

H v Griffiths (2009): the presumption in favour of *mens rea* can be seen as a constitutional principle.

Duguid v Fraser (1942): *mens rea* is the norm in all offences and it is for the Crown to establish that it does not apply in an individual case. Strict liability is most likely to be found where the offence is *mala prohibita* rather than *mala in se*, and where the statute creating the offence is regulating an issue of social concern.

Lim Chin Aik (1963): if strict liability would not promote greater vigilance in adhering to the terms of the statute, it is unlikely to apply.

Henvey v HM Advocate (2005): the word "possession" has been interpreted to require the *mens rea* of knowledge.

Mackay Brothers v Gibb (1969): the word "permit" has been interpreted to require knowledge on the part of the accused. Wilful blindness to an obvious fact is sufficient to constitute this knowledge.

Mitchell v Morrison (1938): the word "cause" (as in failing to cause a correct record of hours worked to be kept) has been interpreted as importing strict liability.

INDEX